Henrie de Bornier

The Romance of a Playwright

Henrie de Bornier

The Romance of a Playwright

ISBN/EAN: 9783744675253

Printed in Europe, USA, Canada, Australia, Japan

Cover: Foto ©Thomas Meinert / pixelio.de

More available books at **www.hansebooks.com**

THE ROMANCE

OF A

PLAYWRIGHT

BY

VTE. HENRI DE BORNIER

From the French
BY
MARY McMAHON

———

New York, Cincinnati, Chicago:

BENZIGER BROTHERS,

Printers to the Holy Apostolic See,

1898

CONTENTS.

PART FIRST.

PART SECOND.

THE ROMANCE OF A PLAYWRIGHT.

Part First.

CHAPTER I.

THE OPENING OF THE CHASE.

PREFECTS are not always fortunate; their ambition is satisfied with occasional good luck. On the first Sunday of September, 1878, the Prefect of Tours considered himself very unfortunate. He and his neighboring colleagues had fixed upon that day for the opening of the chase; on the morning of this day, so impatiently looked forward to, a gentle, persistent rain set in and continued till the following Sunday—a week of a steady rain, unceasing and pertinacious, like the weary loquacity of a dull, prosy orator. This is why the Marquise de Rillé's guests were not extravagantly cheerful on this afternoon of the second Sunday of September, 1878.

They had all driven over to the neighboring village to Mass in the morning, execrating all the way the miniature deluge which discolored and marred the beauty of the little twelfth-century church, with its sixteenth-century spire and doorway. They returned to Rillé Castle in the same beautiful weather, but this half-hour drive scarcely sufficed to clear away the clouds from the brows of the disappointed huntsmen. Breakfast, however, brought an agreeable diversion. Guests are generally more cheerful and in better humor at breakfast after Mass; they bring home better thoughts suggested by what they have seen and heard, and good thoughts always light up the countenance. Then, even among pious, reverent Christians, Mass furnishes subject for discussion. They could not fail to observe the unfashionable toilettes of the mayor's wife and daughters; that the schoolmaster sang out of tune, and the *Domine, salvam fac Rempublicam* grated painfully on their ears; and the curé's sermon—what a theme for comment! Were there not direct allusions to

this one and that one, indirect reproaches, les-
sons addressed to whom they concerned? Did
not the good curé go a little too far in attacking worldly luxury so violently, and anathematiz-
ing extravagant toilettes? The curé is a saint,
but he is certainly rather severe. Breakfast
over, the guests separate, some going to the
drawing-room, others to play billiards; for the
rain still continues. It is a protecting rain to
the hares and partridges; the guests must re-
sign themselves to their disappointment. The
men smoke at their game of billiards, the ladies
gather round the large table in the drawing-
room; but, as it is Sunday, fancy-work is not
allowed—they cannot even knit for the poor.
Reading being permitted, some one reads aloud
the *Gazette de France;* the literary *feuilleton*
meets with entire approval, the rare talents and
exquisite grace and elegance of the author prove
an inexhaustible theme. Then the conversation turns to Paris of former times; here was
cause for universal pleasure and approbation,
but when everybody is of the same opinion
conversation soon flags—the men as well as
the women being Loyalists, there was no

opportunity for the least discussion. Oh, if they only had one small Republican to demolish!

The rain still holds on, dismal as the countenances of the twelve or fifteen people who watch it fall. It formed a lake around the castle, it rained on the trees, and still more under the trees, and a member of the Institute hazarded this quotation from Virgil: "*Bis pluii in silvio.*" * This erudite Latin citation only increased the general gloom. It was too much!

Suddenly the Marquise de Rillé, breaking the oppressive silence, resumed the conversation.

"My dear friends," said she in her sweet, clear voice, "you must admit that you are all fearfully bored."

"Oh, madame! Oh, aunt! Oh, cousin!" they all exclaimed.

"Yes, I see that you are tired and disappointed; it is my fault, for I have not provided entertainment enough for you. However, I shall try to do so now; wait a moment." So saying, she tripped lightly out of the room.

Madame de Rillé, despite her sixty years,

* It rains twice in the woods.

still retained her shapely figure; her pale, calm face was crowned with beautiful white hair, and her grave, handsome eyes sparkled with intelligence and kindly benevolence. She was a childless widow, but this did not prevent her loving tenderly—rather a rare thing in this world—a host of nieces, nephews, and cousins.

She returned in a few moments, holding in her hand a small square box, which, with a mysterious air, she placed on the table.

"What have you there? what have you there?" asked the young women.

"You will see, children."

She then opened the box, the inside of which was a sort of chess-board, divided into numerous squares.

"Examine it well, and then listen," said the marquise. "Nearly three years ago I saw a grand metrical drama played in Paris. The action was laid in the time of Charlemagne, and the piece opened with a scene which seemed to me very curious: the actors played 'The Game of Virtues.' This game, unknown to our contemporaries, even to the ladies, is very simple: The names of thirty-six virtues are written on a chess-board; one of the players throws a die at a venture on the board, and pledges himself to practise, during one or several days, the virtue designated by the throw of the die. They may even throw several times, and then there will be several virtues to prac- tise. I was seized with the desire to procure one of these chess-boards, and made search in all the shops where antiques were sold. But 'The Game of Virtues' had become obsolete, and my search was in vain. I still held to my idea, however, and with the aid of my cabinet-maker I have manufactured one of these boxes. Look, on each of the thirty-six squares I have written, with my own hand, the name of a virtue. It is true, there are only three theological virtues, but, with the subdivisions, I succeeded in completing the necessary number of thirty-six. This, then, is 'The Game of Virtues,' and I propose that we make use of it to-day; it will certainly be more amusing than watching the rain fall."

" Oh, yes !" all replied eagerly.

" Well, then, let us begin. But to prevent

confusion, there will be at first only two players, and I shall select them myself. Those, however, who are not playing must watch, encourage, and help the players in the practice of the virtue that falls to their lot. This being understood, I choose my charming cousin, Marie Poncette Morel, and my handsome nephew, Robert de Salemberry. Come forward, Poncette; come, Robert." A young woman and a tall young man stepped out of the group.

"Poncette," said the marquise, "take the dice-box from the backgammon-table, put one of the dice in it (one is enough); now throw it on 'The Game of Virtues,' without looking." Poncette smilingly obeyed and threw the die as she was directed. The marquise carried the chess-board to the window, the better to read it, and returned, saying:

"The virtue designated by your throw is: 'Avoid ridiculing your neighbor!'"

Had the marquise read aright? Did she not cheat a little, or aid the venture by her perspicacity? Who knows? At all events, the company exclaimed in chorus, with a laugh which seemed to say, " The reading of the cast is clever."

Poncette Morel blushed slightly, but soon recovered her self-possession, and said with a smile :

" I shall find it difficult, but I'll try. How long must I practise this little virtue?"

" Let us make it a fortnight," replied Madame de Rillé. " And each time that you fail in the practice of it, my dear child, you will give me five hundred francs for my poor. You are rich."

" I fear I may not be at the end of the fortnight."

" That is your affair. Now it is my nephew's turn, the great and celebrated poet, Robert de Salemberry. Throw the die, Robert."

The marquise took the box to the light as before, and returned from the window, saying :

" This is the virtue fate imposes on my dear nephew: 'Repair the injury that has been done.' "

" Fate is mistaken this time; I have nothing to repair."

" We shall see about that later, my handsome

nephew. Take time to reflect upon it, to examine carefully, and judge yourself conscientiously. For the present we shall occupy ourselves with my dear Poncette; in a fortnight, when she has gone through this trial, difficult enough for her, I fear, we shall think of you, Robert. This is what is expected: From this moment, Marie Poncette Morel is to endeavor, God helping, under the eyes and in the judgment of her friends and relations, to practise the particular virtue allotted her."

This is the way the Marquise de Rillé's guests in September, 1878, opened the chase of the virtues, which consoled them to a certain extent for not being able to chase hare, deer, and partridge.

CHAPTER II.

CHANCE, aided or corrected by the clever dowager, had struck home. Madame Marie Poncette Morel had but one fault, but she had a full complement of that one: it was a mania for ridiculing others. This cruel propensity in which she took pleasure was hers naturally and by education. It was her way of being cheerful and amusing. Yet she had reason enough to be sad.

Madame Morel was the widow of a banker of Tours, who married her when she was only sixteen, partly for her pretty face, but chiefly for her handsome fortune; and at eighteen she was the most unhappy of pretty women. Shamefully deceived by her husband, she endured it at first, for she was proud and hid her sorrow; but, unfortunately, this hidden chagrin soon changed into bitterness, which made her look upon all

16

men with a sort of contemptuous pity, believing them all to be formed upon the model of the inconstant, volatile M. Morel. She was clever, and used her wits freely in ridiculing the foibles, faults, eccentricities, and even the misfortunes of that sex which, according to the grammar, is nobler than the feminine.

She took special delight in the sufferings of certain married men, and their misfortunes were the occasion of her keenest witticisms. Although perfectly correct herself, she was most indulgent towards frivolous women, because of the annoyance they caused their husbands; not wishing to revenge herself on her own spouse, she would, at least, take revenge on those born under an evil star, and it seemed to her that M. Morel received a vague reflex, as it were, of the fatal planet. Her perfect sense of honor and her religious principles permitted her no other retaliation. M. Morel, however, ended his days better than he had lived; he was killed in the war of 1870.

A widow at twenty, without pretending to display any more grief than she felt, Poncette determined to tempt fate no more, to remain a

widow and to enjoy the pleasure expressed in
the poet's verse : " *Suave mari magno—*" *

All that remained to her of her marriage was
an invincible tendency to ridicule husbands, and,
in her eyes, all men were husbands ; they have
been, she would say, they are, or they will
be ! Among those whom she most wilfully
ill-treated was Baron Louis de Nolongue, a
distant cousin of hers and also of her hostess,
the charming dowager whom we have just
depicted.

Baron Louis de Nolongue had a painfully sad
history, and a more merciful cousin would not
have been so cruel as to laugh at ·it. An or-
phan from his early youth, without guide or
counsel, he made a very foolish outset in life.
At nineteen he married a German several years
his senior, and very much less unsophisticated.
After a few months of married life, she longed
for the windmills on the banks of the Spree,
thinking, perhaps, that she would not find

---

* " Suave mari magno turbantibus æquora ventis,
E terra magnum alterius spectare laborem."

—*Lucretius ii., 1.*

" 'Tis pleasant, when the seas are rough, to stand
And see another's danger, safe at land."

enough windmills in France upon which to throw all her caps.*

There was a scandal, a lawsuit, a legal separation, and then one fine day the blond Gretchen died. Her husband was the only one who wept for her, for he did weep! One of the mysteries of the masculine heart is this nervous sensibility which seizes and overcomes it at the death of an unworthy wife, if the guilty one has ever been loved, were it but for a day. The tears Louis de Nolongue could not hide were recorded in heaven, but the world laughed at them. As to Poncette, she laughed openly at his grief; it was the first cheerfulness she had shown since the conventional mourning of her widowhood.

Such frivolous women are not mourned very long. M. de Nolongue retained only the scar of the double wound inflicted by his marriage and the death of his unworthy spouse. There are fatalities in life. Three or four years later, Louis de Nolongue, whose heart was too tender to remain empty, fell in love again—and with

* A French proverb: "Jeter son bonnet par-dessus les moulins." To defy public opinion.—[TRANSLATOR.

whom? None other than his scoffing cousin,
Poncette Morel. He asked her hand through
Madame de Rillé, but Poncette refused him
very decidedly, preferring to remain a widow.
She could not, however, miss such a splendid
opportunity of venting her ironical sallies,
which were like an explosion of fireworks; it
would be impossible to relate all that she in-
vented in the way of sharp epigrams, spiteful
allusions, and petty innuendoes. Louis de Nolongue felt all this keenly, but he suffered in
silence, confiding his tribulation only to his
cousin, Robert de Salemberry, who consoled
him as best he could; unfortunately, for certain sorrows there is no consolation.

Poncette was not, however, malicious; if she
had had any idea of the torture she inflicted on
her cousin, she certainly would have deprived
herself of this small pleasure, for, strange as
it may seem, she was really not bad at heart.
Moreover, she was fully convinced from the
first that chance, or Madame de Rillé's cleverness, had contrived by this "Game of Virtues"
to teach her a lesson, and the laughter of her
friends on this occasion made her feel that per-

haps the lesson was deserved; but as she had no intention of enriching the poor in whom the marquise was interested, Poncette resolved to be on her guard and to restrain her habitual railleries.

During the entire day she went about among the marquise's guests, making herself equally agreeable to both ladies and gentlemen, saying something pleasant to each in the most gracious tone and with the most winning smile. She continued in this charming mood at dinner and all through the evening. In vain were snares laid for her; they only afforded her an opportunity of practising her new virtue. The conversation was vainly turned on subjects likely to rouse her spirit of raillery; she withstood the almost irresistible temptations, giving serious, well-considered replies to the most insidious questions. When asked what she thought of the Marquis de X.'s prolonged stay in Paris, she answered, with apparent conviction: "M. de X. is having a work on political economy published, upon which he has labored for ten. years, with the aid and advice of one of the professors of the College of France."

Up to ten o'clock, the solemn hour at which they all separated, Poncette's brilliant triumph was deservedly admired by all. Just as she was about to leave the room she approached the marquise, and handing her a pocket-book said :

" My dear cousin, there are five hundred francs. And now I am going to tell you the name of our friend M. de X.'s collaborator : she is called Eulalie Réséda Finemouche. Polichinelle told me this secret."

And taking her malachite candlestick from the mantel, she fled from the room, and her merry laugh echoed through the long corridors of the Castle de Rillé.

" Never mind," said the marquise, accompanying her guests as they separated for the night ; " the good seed is sown, and the soil is not too bad."

CHAPTER III.

THE DRAMA OF SIX PERIWIGS.

SEVERAL days after the scene just related, Louis de Nolongue sat smoking and chatting with his cousin Robert de Salemberry on the terrace of the pretty little cottage that Louis had recently built, within a short distance of Rillé. He had a talent for building, and frequently indulged in his favorite occupation by constructing in various places small castles and country-houses, of which, however, he soon grew tired. This one, called Les Chartrettes, in memory of Gabrielle d' Estrèe, did honor to his taste and architectural knowledge. It was a perfect little jewel-case, a nest for a bride and groom; and lacked nothing but the pink and white gowns fluttering in and out of the paths in the little park that ran down to the bank of the Lathan, the only river in this, it must be admitted, rather arid country.

The thought of what it lacked, doubtless,

occurred to Louis de Nolongue, for he said to his cousin:

"I am very proud of my little house, but it is very lonely here."

"That sigh is for the sprightly Poncette, is it not?"

"You know well it is."

"Everybody knows it, and no one better than she."

"Oh, my friend, how can they be so beautiful, and yet so cruel?"

"Oh, yes; those qualities go together."

"She not only does not love me, but she ridicules me with a spitefulness that rends my heart."

"But she has not, at least, within the last few days."

"That is because of 'The Game of Virtues,' in which she is determined not to lose too much. But the term expires in about twelve days; then she will take her revenge, and I know I shall pay for the past with usury."

"It will be your own fault then, my dear Louis."

"Why so?"

"You make such a feeble defence. You do not even try to defend yourself. You submit to be trampled upon by this scoffer, instead of answering her in the same vein; yet you are no simpleton."

"Answer her! I contend with her! I would rather attack a wild boar with a parlor-pistol."

"You are mistaken; by taking fair, direct aim, the smallest ball may be sent straight to the heart."

"I doubt very much if she even has a heart."

"A woman always has; it is for us to touch it."

"That is easy enough for you, thanks to your refined masculine beauty, your intellect, reputation, and genius."

"Do not speak of my genius!"

"But every one speaks of it."

"If it is spoken of a hundred years hence, I might tell you if there was reason for it," replied de Salemberry, smiling. "Let us talk of your affairs; that is better. I repeat you are too timid with this malicious Poncette. I'll wager you have not told her that you love her."

" I asked her hand through Madame de Rillé."

" You ought to ask her yourself."

" That would be suicide. "

" No, a duel."

" With very unequal weapons!"

" One never knows.   Well, promise me one thing, my dear Louis: Poncette is coming with the other ladies to visit your country-seat; if she attacks you, promise me to defend yourself."

" I'll try."

" Courage, then, courage!"

" You are right, Robert; I will be courageous."

" Good! well, here they come; be brave!"

" Yes, yes; I begin to tremble already."

Poncette arrived a little in advance of Madame de Rillé, who was accompanied by a number of young ladies of the neighborhood.   Louis went forward to meet her with that refined grace of which even his timidity could not rob him.   The ladies had walked through the fields

following the river, which flows clear and lim-
pid under the tall willows, from the woods of
Champ-chevrier.

Nothing affects the mind and soul more
agreeably than a walk on a bright, sunny day
in the midst of the mysterious joys of nature,
which awaken similar secret joys in mind and
soul; a gentle grace seems to rain upon us from
heaven; and if we meet a friend at the end of
the road, the mutual greeting is apt to be both
gracious and cordial. The meeting between
Louis and his charming visitors on this occasion was most cordial and animated. None of
the ladies had yet seen Les Chartrettes; for, as
the poet refuses to read his poems in fragments,
so Louis' self-love prevented his exhibiting his
work until entirely completed. Great was the
enthusiastic admiration expressed by the ladies
at sight of the little castle.

" It is a Swiss châlet," said the marquise.

" Larger than those at Interlaken, fortunately," added Poncette, clapping her hands ;
" shall we hear the '*Ranz des Vaches,*' cousin?"

" Alas! no."

"I'll play it for you on the piano, if there is one."

"Yes, by all means."

M. de Nolongue, followed by the ladies, ascended the steps of the castle, and, opening the door, entered the vestibule, the walls of which were profusely ornamented with some thirty stag-horns.

At sight of all these cynegetic trophies, Poncette, looking at the master of the house, exclaimed: "Oh! oh! oh!"

M. de Nolongue shuddered, but, as Poncette confined herself to these three exclamations, he breathed freely and led the way to the dining-room, where luncheon was served. The ladies did honor to the delicious cream and luscious peaches offered them, and moistened their lips in cups of foaming Vouvray, the native wine of Touraine and Anjou. Poncette, raising her glass, said, graciously:

"To our good and loyal friend, the host of Les Chartrettes!"

The host, much flattered, returned thanks with emotion.

"Now," resumed Poncette, "my dear cousin,

you must gratify our curiosity by showing us every part of the castle."

Louis did not wait to be asked a second time, but threw open all the doors, and the guests admired the elegance of the drawing-room, the comfortable smoking-room, which also served as a library, and the billiard-room with its severe luxury, also several bedrooms on the first floor, apparently awaiting numerous guests.

Having sufficiently admired everything, they returned to the drawing-room, but Poncette lingered behind, standing motionless before the only door that M. de Nolongue had not opened.

She remembered that Louis at this point had turned aside and showed unusual eagerness to lead his visitors quickly past this door, which had neither lock nor key, nor the slightest indication of any kind of knob. This puzzled Poncette, and she began to examine the mysterious door. "Could it be a blind door?" she asked herself; no, for a ray of light underneath showed that there was a window opposite on the inside. By close scrutiny, Poncette discovered, not on the door itself, but at one side, hidden in a groove of the wainscoting, a small metal disc.

She immediately recalled having noticed in her
cousin's room a small copper key in a little
onyx cup.   Poncette was naturally curious; on
this occasion she was very indiscreet.   Without
a moment's reflection, she tripped lightly into
Louis' room, and returned with the key in question.   "This must be it," she said to herself,
and quickly applied the key to the small disc.
The door flew open, and Poncette was convulsed
with laughter, for this was what she saw:

On six knobs, or rather pegs, fastened to the
wall, were spread out six blond periwigs, frizzed
and curled exactly alike.

"Louis is wearing the seventh," exclaimed
Poncette; "one for every day in the week, and
no one suspected it."   The periwigs were perfect marvels.   Poncette was again seized with
a fit of nervous laughter, but stopped suddenly,
for Louis de Nolongue had just entered the
room.   He closed the door behind him, his pale
face betraying great agitation, and approached
his cousin trembling.   He feared that this discovery had ruined all his hopes, but, remember-
ing Robert's advice, he thought that all might
yet be gained.

"Very well," said he, in a suppressed tone of voice; "yes, laugh, cousin, laugh at me; it is true I have this misfortune, I am guilty of this folly; I am bald as Cæsar, and I try to conceal it. I am absurd; you may laugh. I thought I had taken every precaution to prevent discovery, and you will laugh still more at this: I had them secretly brought from England, and believed no one would know anything about it. Now everybody will know it, for you could not resist the pleasure of telling, and I shall be more ridiculous than ever. But you will be happy; yes, very happy; you are so malicious. I know you; go! No, I am wrong; I insult you by speaking thus. Forgive me; pardon me!" Louis fell on his knees before Poncette and seized both her hands.

"Rise, cousin; I forgive you."

"No, cousin; I do not deserve to be forgiven. I have something more still to reproach myself with, and you will have very good reason to laugh this time. But I will tell you all. I love you, I love you, I love you! madly, foolishly; but I love you. But what matters it? I have suffered so much already, I

can suffer still more. Ah, if you knew how
your ridicule and disdain are killing me; but I
love you despite it all. I love you tenderly;
and why? Perhaps because you also have suffered; and I sometimes hope that of our two
sorrows we might perhaps make one happiness.
Yes, it is absurd; I know it; but I have dreamed
of it; and see, I weep like a child at the thought
that this dream has vanished forever. All is
over for me; you have thought me ridiculous,
now you will consider me grotesque. Nevertheless, Poncette, I love you from the very
depths of my soul. Put no restraint upon yourself; laugh, and make others laugh at my expense. Tell all that you have just discovered;
do not spare me, be more malicious than ever;
betray my absurd secret; have no remorse; betray me!"

"Cousin," replied Poncette, "I am an honest
woman, and would not betray my husband."

A fortnight after this incident, Madame Marie
Poncette Morel married the Baron Louis de
Nolongue.

CHAPTER IV.

A PLAYWRIGHT'S REVENGE.

THE day after this marriage, which was cele-brated with great pomp, the Marquise de Rillé brought together at a wedding-feast the char-acters whom we have already met at her house during that memorable rainy week that inter-fered with the pleasures of the chase. Dinner was finished just at nightfall, and the marquise addressed the company thus:

"My dear children," said she, smiling with a certain degree of pride, "you are all convinced, by a notable example, of the efficacy of 'The Game of Virtues.' Do you not think so, Madame de Nolongue?"

"Certainly," replied Poncette, with a slight blush.

"Then let us continue this very useful experi-ment. It is now my nephew Robert de Salem-berry's turn. You know the game allotted to him a virtue difficult enough to practise: to *repair the injury that has been done.* From this moment he ought to study this command seriously and practise it conscientiously. Begin, then, my dear nephew, without delay. We have given you a fortnight's respite; you have had time to reflect and to prepare your weapons for this conflict with yourself."

" But, my dear aunt, I told you two weeks ago that I have nothing to repair, never having done an injury to anybody."

Madame de Rillé looked Robert full in the face for a moment in silence, and then said, deliberately :

" Stephen de Fleurigny."

" Oh! as to that," replied Robert, petulantly, " you know well that I was in the right."

" So you say, my dear nephew, but one is apt to be a bad judge of his own case. Be that as it may, go, smoke your cigar in the park, and examine your conscience. Go, my dear poet, go!"

" With pleasure, my dear aunt, but my examination of conscience is already made."

" Make it again."

" May I take Louis with me?"

"What! separate a bride and groom of yesterday? No, indeed. Moreover, Louis' presence might interfere with your remorse, if you have any."

"I shall not have any, my dear aunt."

"Go and see, my dear."

Let us follow Robert in his solitary walk, and profit by it to become better acquainted with the man who is to be the principal character in our story.

While walking under the tall trees, gently stirred by the evening breeze, many memories involuntarily arose in the young man's mind. One of the most apparent and curious facts, phenomena, if you wish, of our epoch, in which there is so much that is curious, is certainly the importance that writers have acquired. If there is a class of men who have profited largely by the extension of modern liberty, it is the class of great literary men, and sometimes even those of lesser merit. He who first made use of the term, "kings of thought," employed an ambitious, perhaps, but a perfectly true expression. They are, in fact, veritable kings; they have their court of enthusiastic admirers, thurifers, chamberlains, chroniclers, historiographers. Like kings, they have their budget, for glory and reputation are of little value in these days without riches. The press, romance, the theatre, all enrich genius, and even simple talent, and the rights of the author have become as obvious a truth as, at least, many of the political charters. Against this royalty, defended by the formidable army of public opinion, nothing avails. While public opinion is with them, famous writers have nothing to fear; struggles, hatred, injustice, calumnies, prosecution and exile but add to their strength, by multiplying the echoes that repeat their name to all people in all parts of the world.

This royalty, like the others, falls or perishes only by its own faults.

What, then, are these faults?

Rather would we break the pen that writes these lines, than ever diminish, outrage—above all, grieve these masters, these sovereigns of human thought. But truth is not an outrage, to measure is not to diminish; and it is permitted to do in the literary order as our fathers did in the political order: to write at the head of a book these bold but respectful words, "Remonstrance to the King."

This said, let us state and designate the rock upon which this literary royalty is apt to run. It is pride. Why should not the souls of these public favorites be imbued with pride? A man must needs possess very superior virtue to remain modest in the midst of this concert of eulogy, adulation, and hyperbole, and not be intoxicated by the captivating perfume of all the censers swung before him. As long as this pride is gratified, it is easy for him to appear smiling and amiable in his gold and azure nimbus. If he is wounded, he suddenly becomes terrible. Such was the case with our hero.

Robert de Salemberry seemed to have been born under the luckiest star. Descended from an ancient, noble family of Navarre, rich, handsome, possessed of brilliant intellect and calm temperament, he realized to a wonderful degree Auguste Barbier's description of the type of the "artist with tranquil brow and hands of fire." Robert had but to enter the world to win it. At twenty he made his *début* in a poem as strange as its title: "All the Tombs." It was a medley of epopee, elegy, lyrics, philosophy, and romance; at times melancholy, then suddenly gay; abounding in faults of taste, audacious theories, inflammable ideas, excessive sentiment; but such power and strength were apparent through the entire poem that a critic wrote of it, " There lurks a lion in this thicket," which described it well.   The poem was signed simply with the name Salemberry, the author believing that this sonorous, mysterious name was made for fame; and he was not mistaken. It won renown, restricted as yet to a circle of literary men.   But Salemberry wanted something better than this—great public celebrity— and he acquired it through romance and the drama.

Salemberry's novels were no less faulty than his first poem, but they were happy faults; too many details and descriptions, too much useless analysis and subtlety, too much brushwood, as in the poem; but here, also, the presence of the lion was felt.

It was to the theatre especially that Salemberry owed his celebrity.   He was born for the drama; comedy and grand tragedy flowed

in his veins. Even in his comedies the tragic
author was revealed. His plays met with
brilliant success, and the poet tasted the
inebriating joys of a daily renewed popular-
ity. Strangely enough, after a brief period of
vertigo, Salemberry himself recognized what his
talent lacked. When his more or less sincere
flatterers exclaimed, "Admirable! sublime!
splendid! a masterpiece!" the poet said to
himself: "No, no! I have not achieved a masterpiece yet, but I will accomplish one, and
soon."

An unexpected event prevented him, at least
for a time, from carrying out his laudable design.

A small newspaper, called *The Viper*, had
recently been started, and it did not belie its
name. Its self-imposed mission consisted in
stinging all who came within its reach.
Whether this was done through pure malice, or
for revenge or pleasure, was unknown, but the
fact that it would sting was evident. When a
man was strong and healthy these stings were
easily cured—a few drops of alkali sufficed.
Nevertheless, the memory of them remained,
and also the fear of other and more serious

bites; for, despite the proverb, "Kill the beast," the poison is not eradicated.

The Viper one fine day stung our, up to that time, triumphant and indemnified hero. An anonymous article attacked de Salemberry's talent, and spoke rather slightingly even of his character. But there was nothing outrageous in it for which he could demand an account; the critic adroitly mingled eulogy with appreciation of the celebrated poet's works, and concluded with these words: "To those who will say his style is very dull, we would simply answer: Yes, but dulness from above."

Salemberry was accustomed to much less acidulated praise; he knew well that if this trenchant remark should spread and obtain credence, he would soon be classed among the most solemn and soporific pontiffs; a flattering pontificate, but scarcely to be envied. Salemberry could, however, have easily overlooked this disagreeable flattery, considering the criticism unjust and untrue, as it really was; but *The Viper* contained something more—this perfidious quotation: "*The duchess' pears are not*

the least tender!" This was an allusion to an
event in the private life of our hero. There
was nothing to be said in the matter; he could
make no defence; the remedy would have been
worse than the evil. He wondered who could
be the author of the article, but was unsuccessful in his efforts to discover. He was not aware
that he had any enemies, and believed that his
most intimate friends were ignorant of this secret of his early life. Moreover, the affair to
which this phrase referred was now a thing of
the past. His efforts to discover the author
of this malicious attack were all the more fruit-
less owing to the need of the great discretion
to be used in the search.

But the article in *The Viper* went farther
than Salemberry supposed. One evening in
the foyer of the theatre he had a box of can-
died fruit which he offered to those about him.
As he handed the box to a celebrated soubrette,
he said gallantly:

" The apple for you, as the most beautiful."

" The pear for you," she replied archly.

Salemberry blushed slightly, and she, per-
ceiving it, added:

" Shall I be indiscreet, my dear, if I tell you the author of that article? But you know it perfectly well."

" No, I assure you, I do not."

" Play the innocent! It is the secret of Europe and America."

" The name, I beg of you."

" Stephen de Fleurigny."

" Nonsenfe! that is absurd; he is my most intimate friend."

" Oh, very well then."

" My dear child, you may say to Europe and America that it is the most unqualified calumny."

" Very generous of you, my great poet! "

Salemberry made no further reply, and went away indignant, but thoughtful.

He had known Stephen from early youth, and considered him his most faithful and devoted friend. They met first at Rillé, where Stephen lived with his mother and his little sister, Gilberte. As boys they attended the same college, and later continued their studies together at the same English university. In 1870 they enlisted in the same regiment of

Zouaves, and, finally, the similarity of their tastes in poetry and the arts united them still more closely.

Aside from this, their natures were absolutely different: Robert was the lion, as described by the critic of whom we have already spoken; Stephen was the gazelle.

Stephen de Fleurigny, with his fair hair, deep blue eyes, calm pale face, handsome figure, and hands of a prelate, seemed a living image of refined religious poetry. Among the poets of a generation that numbers many great and noble ones, Stephen held a place apart. His strong, clear odes had the grace of the Lombardy poplar, that murmurs so softly in the breeze. He wrote tender elegies, that all the women knew by heart like their mother tongue. His marvellously chaste sonnets resembled those Greek figures which seem to stretch forth their arms but to offer flowers in marble and alabaster urns. Stephen's fame was neither pronounced nor widespread, but he had discreet and faithfully devoted admirers. It was not the ocean with its tempests and broad horizon, but a lake peacefully sheltered by green hills, and skimmed

by fleet skiffs in which lovers sang while contemplating the twinkling stars.   Stephen was
satisfied with this quiet fame, and was loved all
the more in the susceptible world in which he
lived, that he sought neither the trumpeted success nor the material profit of a literary life.

Robert de Salemberry thought of all this on
leaving the theatre; the accusation made against
his friend had wounded him like a dagger-thrust.

" It is impossible," said he aloud, regardless
of the passers-by; " it is impossible!   The world
is decidedly base and cowardly to listen to and
believe such monstrous things; I will not even
think of it."

On reaching home Robert opened his desk,
and taking out a package of Stephen's letters
began to read them over.   Stephen spoke rarely
of himself in the letters, always of his friend,
and in the most tenderly affectionate and broth-
erly manner, mingling with the wisest counsels
the profoundest esteem and admiration.   He
applauded each success achieved by Salemberry,
and sounded his praises far and near with almost
childlike pleasure.

" What a valiant heart," said Robert to him-

self, as he read. "And this is the man they
accuse. If I ever discover the propagator of
this servants' gossip, I shall lengthen his ears,
the better to cut them off."

The concluding sentence of one of the letters
attracted Robert's attention for some time:

"My dear chum," wrote Stephen, "now that
I have seriously lectured you on your poetry and
prose, let me give you a bit of advice: be wiser
than Solomon and David; and if you have any
secrets other than poetical ones, do not confide
them to me, for you know I am very puri-
tanical. Adieu, great brother, until we meet
again."

Robert examined carefully the date of this
letter: October 17, 1872.

"This is strange," thought he; "the date coin-
cides with that on which I committed my greatest folly. But Stephen knew nothing of it,
nor did anybody else. If any one knew it, it
was very evidently the editor of *The Viper*.
Chance has served the rascal well; chance being
often a rascal himself."

Robert continued and finished the reading of
the letters with ever-increasing emotion.

"O earth!" he exclaimed, as he finished them, "a great poet had good reason to call you the throne of folly! I would add, throne of calumny.   Stephen is an angel of friendship."

Though Robert went to bed and slept on this good thought, he was suddenly awakened by a feeling of sharp pain—having dreamed that a viper had stung him to the heart, and that a voice called to him, "It is Stephen!"

Robert could sleep no longer, and spent the long hours in thoughtful introspection; the habit of analysis that served him so well in writing a drama or romance clung to him when he wished to study himself.   He began to recognize with despair that a suspicion was insensibly creeping into his heart, and thrust it aside as he would brush away a buzzing fly; but the importunate insect always returned.

"What creatures we are!" he exclaimed; "that was a wicked thought I had just now."

The dawn of a bright day restored his equanimity.

"What the deuce did I dream last night?"

He went at an early hour to breakfast with

Stephen, who received him as usual, cordially and pleasantly.

"It has rained for a week; I have need of light; enter, young sun."

"The sun is old, Stephen."

"It may be at eight in the evening, but not at eight in the morning; it is only ten now. Rise and adorn with your rays the omelette with truffles that Mistress Tempete, my excellent cook, is making in your honor."

"Always a gourmand, Stephen."

"Yes, Robert; like André Doria's cat, a gourmand, and always faithful."

"How do you know that André Doria's cat was faithful and a gourmand?"

"I guessed it while looking at the portrait of André Doria and his cat in the palace of Genoa. I am thinking seriously of writing a sonnet on this historical discovery, and of dedicating it to you."

As they went into the dining-room, Stephen, noticing that Robert seemed depressed, and wishing to divert him, continued while they enjoyed the truffle-omelette:

"Do you know, Robert, there is something

lacking in modern poetry? We have had, or have, Lamartine, Victor Hugo, Alfred de Musset, Auguste Barbier, Coppée, Sully-Prudhomme, Victor de Laprade, Leconte de Lisle, Eugene Manuel, Louis Bouilhet, Soulary, Salemberry, etc.; but we have neither Boileau nor Berchoux; we have neither satire nor gastronomy. I do not aim at being a Boileau—I leave that ambition to one more cruel; but I should like to be a Berchoux."

"Modesty will be your ruin, Stephen."

"As ambition is of others; better modesty, it causes less suffering."

"If you say that for my benefit, Stephen, you are quite right; I am tormented by ambition."

· "I can well believe it; it is limitless."

"I contemplate writing a second poem—modern science, the great works and great inventions shall be the theme."

"I approve; and seriously, my dear Robert, that is your vocation. *Os magna sonaturum*— to voice great things."

"Well, after breakfast I shall give you a synopsis of my poem."

"Very good; Mistress Tempete, the coffee, the coffee, quickly!"

When they had taken their coffee in the smoking-room, Stephen, installing himself in a large armchair, and rubbing his hands like a man preparing for a fray, said, with his sweet smile:

"Now, friend Robert, we are going to demolish that little poem. Begin, and prepare to be very modest, for I propose to do my duty and to be very severe."

Robert read the prologue and argument of the poem, which was formed on a grand scale of about two hundred verses.

When he had finished reading, Stephen remained a moment in thoughtful silence, and then said, hesitatingly at first, like a huntsman beating the thicket, but soon in a firmer tone:

"The movement is certainly very fine, the style and ideas original, and there are some superb verses; but there is one fault, and it is a serious fault."

"What is it?" asked Robert, a little astonished.

4

" It is this—a fault often acquired by writing for the theatre: The audience seeing the play only as a whole, make you think of it only in that aspect. You are not careful; you are even negligent about details; you are satisfied with the first word that occurs to you, provided it is high-sounding and harmonious; finally, you do not put in the fine lines with the pencil, old fellow; you paint with the brush; your style is affected and influenced by stage scenery; and this is a grave fault."

" Ah! 'I paint with the brush;' that is very severe, Stephen."

" It is the truth."

" It is the first time it has ever been said to me."

" And I tell you it, that it may be .the last."

" Oh, oh, doctor!"

" Doctor, if you wish; believe me, the doctrine is good. The great masters——"

" Ah! if you speak of the great masters——"

" It would be an insult to speak of lesser ones in connection with you."

" But, by Hercules! my good Stephen, a

poem is not a sonnet; dabbling in paint is not very brilliant work; and Miéris does not, perhaps, equal Paul Véronèse."

"Omit the perhaps. Miéris in no way equals you. Only remember that, if Véronèse was timid at times, he was always scientific, and never forgot rhythm and harmony."

"I overlook them, then?"

"You despise them; that is what I am finding fault with. Read the poem again, verse by verse, and I shall prove it to you."

"We must postpone that for some other time, my dear Stephen; I have an appointment at the theatre."

Robert rose, slightly agitated, and extended his hand to Stephen; then as he was leaving said:

"By the way, Stephen, do you know what they say?"

"All they say? That must be a great deal."

"You know that article in *The Viper* in which I was so badly treated, that anonymous article?"

"Well?"

"It is said that you wrote it, Stephen."

Stephen laughed outright in his usual frank manner, but Robert did not even smile.

"What! you laugh at this?"

"Why, certainly."

"There is nothing in it to laugh at, however; it is a very serious thing."

"Serious—for whom?"

"For you and for me; and I demand of you——"

"You demand of me——"

Stephen grew deathly pale; he bit his lips, but controlled himself, and continued in a voice trembling with emotion:

"You ask if I am the author?"

"I ask you to deny it."

The blood now mounted to Stephen's temples; he trembled in every limb, and seizing a rare, fragile vase from the table he crushed it in his hand; then, looking his friend full in the face, he pointed to the door:

"M. de Salemberry, leave my house."

"M. Stephen de Fleurigny, I bid you good morning."

Robert rose, moved slowly toward the door, turned and met Stephen's cold glance, then,

bruskly thrusting aside the porter, departed.
He returned to his home in a state of concentrated rage difficult to describe. True, he suffered more from wounded pride than wounded
friendship.

In worldly friendships, but especially among
literary people, there is always one who rules,
who is master, and often despotic. Between
two friends equality rarely exists; the gentler,
the better nature, yields, voluntarily or unconsciously, to the will of the other. A great man
is not a friend in the affection he shows, and
even feels; there is a latent something that
seems like reward for services. He pays for
the admiration he receives by a smile or word,
as a prince bestows honors and rank upon the
brave soldiers who fight for him. What the
great man really loves is the servant of his fame.

Should the servant for an instant forget his
rôle, the friend, the haughty master, reminds
him of it—at first gently, but soon very imperi-
ously. But if the servant revolts, if the head
that bowed so low, and was supposed to be
accustomed to the shade, should suddenly as-
sert itself and claim its share of the sun—as if

this luminary had nothing better to do than to shine on anything obscure—this would be treachery, the crime of high treason.

Robert de Salemberry had all the pride of a great man, although he had not yet achieved that distinction; his pride cried out like the lion suddenly wounded at night by the hunter.

"He dared not deny it!" he exclaimed; "moreover, he could not. I disconcerted him so by my direct thrust he could not say no. The miserable, perfidious wretch! He has always been jealous of me at heart, and I should have seen it had I not been so unsuspicious. The advice he gave me, his manner of criticising my works under pretext of watching over my fame, were but the outpouring of his jealousy and envy. It was so like him to use that expression, 'You paint with the brush!' Now that I think of it, there were some such words in that infamous article: 'Dulness from above.' It takes an intimate friend to polish that sort of diamond, to stamp aright these aphorisms which are afterward circulated in the world as medals. And that other perfidious sentence: 'The duchess' pears are not the least

tender!' That was the most treacherous of all,
and if I had the right—but I have no cause for
a duel. Nevertheless, the wretch must be pun-
ished; and I shall find some better means than a
sword-thrust. This pun on the duchess pears
is so ridiculously silly, it must surely have been
made by that rosewater poet, that sonnet-maker."

Robert contemptuously repeated these words,
" Sonnet-maker, sonnet-maker!" then suddenly
burst into a strident laugh that was almost savage in its bitterness; but his fierce gayety soon
changed into a pensive mood.

That same evening Robert de Salemberry
called on Jacques Alençon, the manager of one
of the large theatres.

" Reserve the month of October for me," said
Robert; "I shall have a five-act play for you."

The manager answered with his blandest
smile.

The next day Robert started for Switzerland.
Three months later he read his five-act play
to the manager, who gave his opinion thus:
" Bravo, dear master. There will be a sensa-
ation in Landerneau. Seven thousand every
evening, and a hundred performances."

CHAPTER V.

"PICHEGRU * STRANGLED!"

THE rehearsals lasted only a month. It was a prose comedy, entitled "The Poisonous Fang"; this was all the public knew of it. The manager, the actors, and employees of the theatre, and, of course, the author, kept the subject and details of the play a most profound secret. But a few discreet comments artfully spread abroad excited public curiosity. It was said to be a violent attack upon a well-known writer, upon whom the author of "The Poisonous Fang" wished to take re. venge.

Nothing more was known of the play; consequently, on the evening of the first performance, the audience, while waiting for the curtain to rise, were on the alert, for there seemed

* Pichegru was a French general who conspired against Bonaparte; he was arrested, but before his trial was found dead in his prison.

to be a smell of gunpowder in the air. All Paris had prepared itself for this occasion as for a cruel feast.

Stephen, to whom a ticket for an orchestra-chair had been sent according to custom, was present at the first representation. He arrived in Paris the previous evening, and felt that he ought not to absent himself, especially as, on account of their quarrel, he had not seen Robert for three months.

The first act disappointed the evil expectations of the public. It was simply a bright, gay scene, at the end of which one of the characters attracted particular attention, although he had very little to say or do; he was a poet who wrote a sonnet in an album and withdrew in silence.

" Look, look! How much that character resembles Stephen de Fleurigny," remarked some of the spectators. " We shall see later what that means." Between the acts this rumor obtained credence, and the curtain rose for the second time on a sea of faces showing eager expectations that were fully realized. The author unmasked his batteries at once. It was a simple scene, in which a poet read a sonnet to a pretty woman.

Why will comic authors take every occasion to ridicule the writers of sonnets? Why should even a poor sonnet be more ridiculous than a bad ode or elegy? Boileau's trenchant verse, "A Faultless Sonnet," is, in a measure, responsible for this. *Oronte's* sonnet in Molière's "Misanthrope" is still more to blame—to say nothing of Mascarille's—in decrying this difficult style of poetry, in which equally as much strength as grace can be displayed. But certain things, like certain men, are unfortunate. The fact is, in spite of the clever sonnet-writers of contemporary literature, the public is always ready to laugh when a sonnet is mentioned, and to murmur almost involuntarily, "A sonnet—it's a sonnet!" Robert de Salemberry knew this well, and he had distilled into this old but ever new scene his most subtle poison. It called forth loud bursts of laughter and shouts of approval from the audience, the women taking part with the author against the character represented. Why was this? We never dared think that French women at times seem like descendants of the implacable Roman Vestals; first, because the Vestals left no direct posterity; and secondly, because French women are better than the Romans of all ages. Nevertheless, it displeases a French woman to hear a ridiculous sonnet addressed to one of her sex. She, doubtless, says to herself, " Such a thing might just as likely happen to me ! " and she revenges herself for the injury which is not, but might be done to her. The women, therefore, displayed their pearly teeth at the reading of the famous sonnet. By this time, all the audience, even those who did not know Stephen, recognized him in the character whom they all condemned.

Success was assured; in the last act it assumed extraordinary proportions. Poor Stephen was torn to pieces like a martyr in the arena. The public became wild at sight of this gladiatorial exploit. Salemberry's name was shouted amidst loud bravos and applause as the curtain fell on this work of vengeance.

Stephen passed out of the theatre between two lines of spectators, who watched him with

malicious curiosity. His face was calm and
grave, and when one of those peculiar friends
with which one is sometimes afflicted asked
him what he thought of the play, he answered
in a tone tinged with sadness :

"I fear Robert may be led by this success into a style that is not naturally his; he is
made for much nobler things."

Meanwhile, Robert, in the greenroom, was
receiving congratulations, hand-pressures, and
embraces, with an indifference which astonished
himself. He was triumphant, but he was not
happy; the revenge of gratified pride is the
most melancholy satisfaction. Robert held his
head high, but to a close observer his absent
manner and clouded brow portrayed a feeling
of extreme dejection.

The famous actress who took the leading
character in his play, Madame Maria Orfano,
was a woman of rare beauty and of great perspicacity. She noticed the dark cloud on the
poet's brow, and, leading him aside, said :

"My dear friend, you are sad; I am myself.
Although I only did my duty in performing my
part in your play, yet I feel quite remorse-

ful.   Think well on this: you are sad; you
have forgotten the ancient Cato's maxim; I
read it this morning in one of my son's school-
books: "'Friendship ought to be gradually sev-
ered, not rent asunder!'"

We shall meet this noble actress again in the
course of this story.   Robert made no reply,
and left the theatre, wishing to be alone.

About two in the morning, two men, passing
under the arcade of the Rue de Rivoli, noticed
a man walking rapidly, beating the air with his
cane, and murmuring between his teeth in a
bitter tone these enigmatical words: " Pichegru
strangled!"

One of the men said, laughing: "There goes
a professor of history, repeating the lesson for
to-morrow.   He cannot be a Bonapartist, for
he decides against Bonaparte in this obscure
question."

The triumphant author awoke next morning
no less melancholy than on the previous evening.
The morning papers brought him reports of his
victory, which was much more brilliant than
he had supposed.   In one of the accounts he
noticed the following:

"No one was ignorant of the real name of the sonnet-writer held up to immortal ridicule by our new Molière. It was Stephen de Fleurigny, but lately his intimate friend. We shall not expatiate on the causes that led to this breach of friendship."

Then the author of the article proceeded to enumerate them in some hundred and fifty lines.

"This is exasperating!" exclaimed Robert; "they go too far. Stephen's offence was against me; I wished to call him to order; that was sufficient. It is unnecessary now to make a Trissotin* of me. These papers always go too far."

The next paper he took up defended Stephen:

"We regret," remarked the critic, "that a noble-hearted, talented man allowed himself to make such an unjust and passionate attack upon an old friend, who is himself a poet of high merit. This mars the work which has just received public applause."

"This is ingenuous," exclaimed Robert, "but

---

* The name of a conceited and by no means brilliant poet, in Molière's "Les Femmes Savantes."

it is the purpose of the play that this gentleman criticises, and he considers me unjust. I shall get even with him some day. If Stephen is likely to have partisans, then I have not sufficiently abused him. After all, I have only done my duty in defending myself and punishing treachery; for he is, no doubt, the author of that anonymous article, and he ought to have acknowledged it. What, then, is there for M. Stephen to complain of? It is true he was ridiculed, and the celebrity he gained thereby he owes to me. The proverb is true, 'Ridicule does not kill.' I know people who have nothing but this to live on."

Robert deceived himself; to do him justice, he was ignorant of the depth and extent of the injury he had just perpetrated. If he could have imagined or foreseen the fatal consequences of his act, his revenge would certainly have appeared odious to him and he would have renounced it.

Stephen had been for several years in love with a young lady, Mlle. Isabelle d'Acérac, whose father was one of the glorious heroes of the Franco-German war. The general would

have much preferred a soldier instead of a poet
for a son-in-law, but Isabelle was of a different
opinion. Stephen's Parisian reputation, his rare
talent, the delicacy of his tender poems, and the
grace of his timid love had won the young girl's
heart. Moreover, she unconsciously took pleasure in the idea of bearing a name already in-
vested with a charm and renown that the future
would augment. She had visions of forming a
salon where the illustrious men of the day would
assemble, of gathering about her works of art,
and celebrities, and, perhaps, of giving tone to
and setting the fashion in the literary world.
This was a very legitimate and pardonable ambition, and one which did not denote a vulgar
mind.

General d'Acérac was a widower with one
son. He could not resist his only daughter,
Isabelle, when she declared that she would marry
no one but Stephen. The alliance, moreover,
was in every way honorable, and the marriage
was decided upon, although not formally announced. The engagement remained a secret
between Stephen, the general, and his daughter.

Stephen loved Isabelle with a rare, profound love. The noble poet's exalted ideals made him place a very high value on his heart; disdaining all sentimental, foolish attachments, he felt that when he once loved it should be for all time. This mystic dreamer was effeminately prudish, and admired those mysterious-hearted widows who looked upon second marriage as a lowering of their nature.

Meeting Isabelle just as she was budding into womanhood, the fiery darts of her sparkling eyes penetrated to the depths of his soul, and awoke a love which was never extinguished.

A few days after the first representation of " The Poisonous Fang," General d'Acérac called upon Stephen.

" My friend," said the general, with military bruskness, " I'll be your second."

" My second!" replied Stephen; "my second —against whom?"

" Against Robert de Salemberry, of course!"

" But, general, I have not the slightest intention of fighting a duel with Robert."

" Nevertheless, you must."

" Why should I?"

5

"Because he has grievously insulted you: because he has covered you with ridicule."

"That is true."

"Well, a good sword-thrust——"

"Pardon, my dear general; be good enough to listen to my reasons. While I might take every precaution to spare my adversary, one never knows how far the point of a sword may reach."

"Very true."

"I might kill Robert; and I do not wish to take that risk. First, because my religious as well as my philosophic principles forbid my fighting a duel; and, finally, because I know no law that condemns a man to death for writing a malicious comedy."

"Well, what reasons!"

"They are very just ones, I assure you."

"But it will be said that you are afraid to fight."

"I proved during the war that I was no coward; and public opinion, the *what will they say?* of the gossips, slander of any kind, or from whatever source, affect me no more than servants' gossip."

"But I am concerned in this. I do not wish
the man whose name my daughter will bear to
be scoffed at in the papers. If you do not
challenge him, I will; and M. Robert de Salemberry shall find at least one of the family
to call him to account. If I am killed, it will
not be very pleasant for you, my boy; and it
will be said, 'There is a gentleman who, unlike
the Cid, allowed his father-in-law to be killed
in his place.'"

"For that very reason, general, I beg you to
do nothing in the matter."

"Very well, then; I shall give you three
days for reflection."

"I do not need to reflect."

"But you need to go to a fencing-academy."

"I have still less need of that."

"Yes, I know—your skill is admirable; but
I cannot understand you; and I warn you that
your conduct will be equally incomprehensible
to my daughter."

"Do you think so?"

"I am sure of it; and if you doubt it, you
have only to discuss the subject with her
briefly, and, as she admires poets, she will say

to you: 'Come forth a victor from a combat of which Chimène is the prize.' Think over this, my dear Stephen; and be assured that I am obliged to take the course I am pursuing. So, good-evening."

General d'Acérac left Stephen, singing as he went away: "Let us guard the safety of the Empire."

The following week the general gave a ball for his daughter's young friends, which Stephen failed not to attend. After one of the quadrilles, the young poet approached Isabelle, and, drawing her aside, said in a low voice:

"You know, Mlle. Isabelle, that your father exacts of me a duel with Robert?"

"Yes, I know."

"And what do you think of it?"

"What do I think——?"

Isabelle hesitated a few moments, then continued:

"You wish to know what I think of it?"

"Certainly."

"Very well, you shall know. Follow me."

They withdrew to the conservatory adjoining the drawing-room, at the lower end of which a quantity of rare plants were so arranged as to form an angular space; this was furnished with · easy-chairs, and at the farther end of the room, behind the flowers, hung Eastern tapestry.

"Go behind these curtains, M. de Fleurigny, and wait."

Stephen obeyed. Isabelle soon returned, followed by several young girls, whom she seated in the angle sheltered by the plants.

"Young ladies," she began, in a grave tone. "I have something very serious about which I wish to consult you."

"Oh, how solemn!" exclaimed Pauline de Meillan.

"You know," continued Isabelle, "that there existed in France, from the twelfth to the fourteenth century, a singular sort of tribunal called the *Court of Love*. Matrons and maidens of high birth assembled to decide certain difficult questions—the import of which the name of the tribunal sufficiently explains. Their judgment was always respected by the lords of that epoch—more chivalrous than ours. Laura de Noves, immortalized by Petrarch, her aunt Phanette, the Countess de Champagne, the

Countess de Flandre, and the Queen, Elenore de Guyenne, took part in this tribunal, which, unfortunately, no longer exists."

"It would have too much to do," murmured Pauline.

"I want you, my dear, clever friends, to re-establish, for this evening, this noble institution."

The curiosity of her young friends being aroused, they all responded enthusiastically to her request.

"This, then, is the question, the problem that I beg of you to solve: May a young lady honorably wed a man who, when insulted, refuses to fight a duel with the man who insults him? Weigh and examine the subject thoroughly, then give your opinion."

"One moment," said Pauline; "let me carefully reflect while finishing my sorbet. Well, I have concluded my reflections."

"Already?" said Mlle. Judith, a fair, rosy-cheeked English girl, who kept raising her sparkling eyes to heaven, from time to time, while pondering over the question.

"My dear Isabelle," replied Pauline, "Judith

is mistaken if she thinks this question requires long deliberation. But there are details and circumstances which must be known before we pronounce judgment. For example, what was the nature of the insult?"

" It was a public insult."

" An overt act?"

" No."

" In words or writing?"

" Both in word and writing."

"Then, in my opinion, the person insulted ought to demand reparation at the point of the sword. And here, my friends, is an example: It is said everywhere that Stephen de Fleurigny is to fight a duel with Robert de Salemberry. And he certainly should, for there never was such an outrageous insult."

"Oh, yes!" exclaimed Mlle. Judith; "how interesting! I sympathize deeply with him, and I sincerely hope he may be the victor."

" But suppose the insulted person of whom we speak does not act as, no doubt, M. Stephen de Fleurigny would under such circumstances?"

" In that case, he would be lacking in honor."

"Then, I put the question again: May a

young lady honorably wed a man who, when outrageously insulted, refuses to fight a duel? Let us put it to the vote. Answer in succession, yes, or no. What do you say, Pauline?"

"No."

"And you, Judith?"

"I refrain from giving my opinion from religious motives."

"And you, Theresa?"

"No."

"And you, Marianne?"

"No."

"You, Elizabeth?"

"No."

"You, Clarissa?"

"No."

"But you, yourself, Isabelle?"

Isabelle, after a moment's silence, answered slowly:

"No."

"One opinion withheld and six noes," said Pauline. "The question is solved, and now to the dance."

The young girls returned to the drawing-room.   A few moments later, Stephen made his escape from the house through the conservatory, unobserved.

Early the next morning Stephen appeared at the French Fencing Academy, where he met Fernan d'Orviedo, one of the most expert swordsmen in Paris, to whom he proposed a trial at fencing.   Stephen parried with such skill, Fernan never succeeded in touching him. Finally, impatiently advancing, he attempted a double disengagement, but Stephen deftly defended himself by a downward parry, warded off the thrust, and, taking direct aim, fairly touched Fernan's breast.

"Hit!" exclaimed Fernan; "you are in excellent trim.   Salemberry will need to look out for himself."

Stephen made no reply, but pressing Fernan's hand left the fencing-hall.   Passing on his way home the church of St. Roch, he hesitated a second before the door, then with bowed head ascended the steps, hesitating again before opening the door, and finally entered.

That same evening General d'Acérac received the following letter:

" GENERAL :

" I relinquish an alliance which was very dear to me. I relinquish it resolutely, but with a broken heart. God must be considered before man. Accept, general, with the expression of my sincere regret, the homage of my respectful attachment.

" STEPHEN DE FLEURIGNY."

The following month Stephen went with his mother and his sister Gilberte to Italy. A short time afterward Isabelle married Pauline's brother, Lieutenant Paul de Meillan, one of her father's ordnance officers. " The Poisonous Fang " was in its sixtieth representation, and soon reached its hundredth. But this success, like all others, ended in time. Salemberry's high order of intellect made him fully comprehend that after so much notoriety he owed the public something better than a work of satirical allusion. He well knew that this was in no way the genial work that had been the dream of his youth and the noble ambition of his desires. He therefore set about finding a subject worthy of the genius he felt surging within him.

He searched a long time, so long that he was still in pursuit of a magnificent ideal at the time this story opens, three years after the triumph he gained by the successful representation of " The Poisonous Fang."

So far his efforts were in vain. This vigorous poet, though still young, seemed suddenly to have become sterile; this was the natural result of the false step he had taken, for raillery and ridicule are to the mind what vice is to the heart. The first nail, once driven, says Alfred de Musset, is drawn out, if ever, only after protracted and terrible efforts. The habit of irony is fatal to great thoughts; a too free indulgence in ridicule intimidates and makes one fear that just restribution here below, that revenge of justice, which sooner or later smites a man with the very weapons he has forged.

While smoking his cigar in the park at Madame de Rillé's, Robert recalled the details of this affair, and, though not saddened by them, he was pensive and preoccupied.

Part Second.

CHAPTER I.

"THE GAZE WAS IN THE TOMB."

"WELL, my dear nephew, have you made your examination of conscience?"

"Yes, my dear aunt, and my conscience is tranquil."

"It must be very easily quieted."

"No; I assure you I have nothing with which to reproach myself."

"What, Robert! Did you not paint poor Stephen in the most grotesque character, vilify him, drag his name in the dust?"

"I did it only in legitimate defence."

"It was the dove, then, that attacked the hawk?"

"Yes, aunt."

"You may say this, and you believe it, I hope; but are you not deceiving yourself?"

"No; I have proof of it—the silence of the offender when questioned."

"What does that prove? That he did not deign to defend himself against such an accusation."

"That was an added insult."

"And his mother and sister, whom you smote with the same blow?"

"Justice strikes blindly."

"Blindness is not her best quality. There are those two poor women who have exiled themselves with your victim; they have now been three years in Rome with Stephen, and I have no one to play whist with me."

"I'll play whist with you."

"You know nothing of the game, but Madame de Fleurigny and Gilberte play remarkably well."

"They will return."

"It would be curious if you should be here when they arrive. I should like to see how you would face them."

"With the countenance of a man who has done his duty."

"What about 'The Game of Virtues,' and

the duty it imposes on you, of repairing the injury done? For, admitting your good faith, you acted no less through anger and spite."

"No, I did justice."

"Like a paladin, did you not? Like the Chevalier Roland, or the Cid?"

"Precisely, my dear aunt."

The drawing-room door opened, and a servant announced:

"Madame and Mlle. de Fleurigny."

"Tableau!" exclaimed Poncette.

"What! is it you, Madame de Fleurigny," cried the marquise; "and you, dear Gilberte; have you fallen from heaven?"

"Yes, from Rome," answered the mother.

"And Stephen?"

"He remains there."

"Now," continued the marquise, "I can have my game of whist. First, let me present you; but it is not necessary; you knoweverybody here. Robert, my handsome nephew, will you kindly prepare the card-table and the accessories, as you call them? That belongs to your province as dramatic author. First come and make your bow to these ladies, and try to resemble Bressant."

Robert, slightly embarrassed, bowed profoundly. Madame de Fleurigny returned his
salutation coldly, Gilberte with indifference.
The young man then arranged everything for
the whist-party.

"Gilberte and I will play against Poncette
and Madame de Fleurigny. Robert, take this
chair by me, and try to profit by our playing
to learn the game, for if there is a bungler at
cards it is you."

The game began. Robert, seated a little
in shadow behind the marquise, faced Gilberte, upon whom fell the light of the green
lamp-shade. He could not help looking
at her, and the thought came suddenly to his
mind :

"It is astonishing how much she resembles
Stephen!"

Robert had not seen Gilberte since what he
in bitter irony called Stephen's "flight into
Egypt," more than three years before. Gilberte
was only sixteen when she left Rillé to go to
Rome. She was then quite a child, and Robert
always looked upon her as such, talking to her
as a brother would to a younger sister, and he

considered her rather ugly, with her long face
and thin shoulders.   This Gilberte bore little
resemblance to the Gilberte of former days.
She was now twenty, tall and graceful, and her
rather elongated, oval face harmonized with the
breadth of her pure, noble brow, crowned with
a rich diadem of blond hair.   But the most no-
ticeable trait was the concentrated, steadfast
expression of her long-lashed, deep blue eyes,
that seemed as if fixed on some object visible
only to herself.   Robert remembered that Stephen's eyes had that same mysterious fixed expression, and the resemblance to her brother in
look and feature was so perfect Robert could
easily imagine that the image of his vanquished
enemy was before him.   Once, Gilberte, laying
her cards on the table raised her head, and opening wide her eyes looked directly at Robert
without seeming to see him.   The young poet,
feeling himself grow red and pale by turns under
her unchanging gaze, rose to escape the unpleasant constraint, but Madame de Rillé soon called
him back, and a shudder went through him as
he again met that same impassable gaze.

Robert, like all poets, knew by heart certain

favorite verses, that he often, almost unconsciously, repeated to himself in a low tone, thus
marking the train of his thoughts, as the soldier
in marching keeps step by humming a well-
known refrain.

Under Gilberte's strange glance, a line from
one of his favorite poems passed rapidly through
his mind; that terrible poem, " The Legend of
the Ages":

" The gaze was in the tomb, and looked upon Cain !"

Robert had never better understood the
depths of its meaning.

Fortunately for him, for he was very ill at
ease, the whist-party soon ended, and Madame
de Rillé's friends withdrew.

Robert accompanied M. and Mme. de Nolongue, who returned on foot to their cottage,
Les Chartrettes.

" What ails you, my dear cousin? " Louis
asked on the way; "you look so sad and
troubled."

" Well he might," added Madame de Nolongue ; "he has seen something worse than
the devil; he met an accusing angel."

6

" What do you mean, my pretty cousin?"

"I mean that Stephen resembles his sister too much ever to have been capable of committing the deed of which you accused him and for which you so cruelly avenged yourself."

" He committed it, nevertheless."

"I do not believe he did anything of the kind, and I hope to convince you of it, my dear cousin. 'The Game of Virtues,' restored to favor by the marquise, has succeeded too admirably with me not to have similar success with you. 'Repair the injury that was done'—this is to be your task, and I shall help you in this difficult undertaking. Louis and I leave to-morrow for Paris; send us a letter of introduction to your great actress, Maria Orfano."

" Why do you want this letter? "

" You will know later."

" You intend to play some trick on me."

" How suspicious you are, sir judge! Send us the letter, and you will have no cause to repent it.' "

" Well, I will, cousin."

" Good! and, while waiting to hear from us,

meditate upon and practise 'The Game of Virtues.' "

As Robert was returning to the castle he saw
Gilberte and her mother some distance down
the road, on their way to the village. On reaching home he went at once to his room, and
before going to bed he chanced to pick up a
collection of poems from various authors; on
opening the volume his glance fell upon the
famous verse:

" The gaze was in the tomb . . .

He threw down the book impatiently, but he
was unable to sleep until far into the night.

CHAPTER II.

THE days following this visit Robert devoted to the chase, and, as Madame de Fleurigny and her daughter came to Madame de Rillé's only during her nephew's absence, Robert did not see Gilberte again till the day on which the following dramatic incident unexpectedly occurred.

On the property belonging to the Rillé estate there was a vast tract of land covered with bare pines and remote from any habitation; the wildest piece of country to be seen in Touraine. It was inhabited solely by a tribe of gypsies whose origin was unknown. Whether they came from Spain, Italy, or Hungary was uncertain, but it was thought they probably were from Spain. The tribe numbered about a hundred men, women, and children. They lived here in defiance of police and keepers, who

84

scarcely dared venture on these wild lands, disdainfully ignored by the officers of the Registry. There was nothing to steal and no one to rob; therefore the gypsies lived by the chase, fishing, and poaching.

Robert often hunted in this neighborhood, abounding in game, the almost complete solitude of which was very pleasant to him.

One day, going through the woods, a black hare started just at his feet, but the underbrush being very thick Robert was obliged to fire at random; it was evident by the excitement and barking of his dog that he had wounded the animal, but it had still strength enough to run, and Robert saw it in the distance making a last effort to reach the heath; but the poor beast did not go far before the dog fell upon it.

Suddenly several men sprang up from behind the bushes, one of whom seized the hare, and, followed by his companions, started for the pine forest that bordered the opposite side of the land. Robert's dog tried to regain possession of his prey, but one of the gypsies struck the dog a blow with a stick that sent it back howling to his master. Robert was furious, and ran after the land pirates, whom he overtook on a narrow path, a few steps from the entrance of the wood. Here he found himself in a clearing, surrounded by several wretched wooden huts. Some twenty dark, savage-looking men and women, hideous in their rags, stood about in menacing attitudes, but Robert was brave.

"Give me that hare," he demanded in a firm voice, addressing the chief of the band.

"It is mine; I found it."

"But I shot it, and it is mine. Give it to me at once!"

Robert advanced aggressively towards his adversary, but in an instant twenty clubs, knives, and hammers were raised over his head. He retreated a few steps, and quickly placing his back against the trunk of a tree he kept the rascals at a distance for a time by rapidly twirling his empty gun.

"Make way with the Christian!" howled all the band.

"Kill him, kill him!" cried a woman who had stealthily crept up behind the young man, and now sprang furiously upon him.

It seemed all over with Robert.

" Stop, Catalina!   Stop, Gualterio!"

The bandits desisted, recognizing Gilberte's voice, who, with her mother, had just come upon the scene.

" Oh, it is the good young lady who cured Pélagia!"

" If I have saved your daughter, Catalina, do me a like favor: protect this young man."

At a sign from Catalina way was made for Robert to pass.

" Take your game," said Gualterio.

" You may have it," answered Robert.

Passing Gilberte, Robert, bowing as he would in a drawing-room, said simply:

" Thank you."

" Go, M. de Salemberry; if you remain the disturbance may be renewed.   Catalina, take me to your daughter; she still needs care."

Gilberte went towards one of the miserable huts, but turned as she was about to enter, and Robert, who looked back at the same moment, met her eyes quietly fixed upon him.

The Marquise de Rillé seemed much amused by the tragic account Robert gave her of his adventure on his return to the castle.

"This was especially arranged for you, my handsome nephew; but it is rather reversing things.   Ariosto would not understand it; Angelica rescues Roger, in this case.   The paladin ought to feel rather humiliated."

"He does, a little, aunt."

"Yes, but that ought not prevent his being grateful.   We shall go together to-morrow to thank Angelica."

"I fear a cool reception."

"Have no fear; a heroine never receives her protégé coldly.   You will offer her a life-saving medal, and all will go well.   You must have looked foolish enough, and she must have been superb, subduing those savages by her commanding voice and manner."

"She was calm and natural, that was all."

"I'll explain this affair to you, my brave nephew.   You have not been much in this part of the country of late years, or you would have known that before they went to Italy, three years ago, Madame de Fleurigny, Gilberte, and Stephen were in the habit of supplying these poor gypsies, who came near killing you, gratuitously with medicine, and almost obliged them to use their remedies. As soon as they heard that one of these rascals had broken an arm or leg, our two infirmarians went at once to their aid, accompanied by Stephen, who is something of a surgeon; which you ought to be also, Robert, for you like to break bones, in a literary sense, though it is better to reset them. Gilberte's specialty was curing the fevers that were very prevalent among the women and children of the tribe. She was always very successful, owing to the use of quinine, and I recommend it to you if you ever have fever. I see that these ladies since their return have resumed their rôle of travelling hospital—fortunately for you. This is the explanation of your adventure."

"Evidently I owe my life to Gilberte."

"Your life, perhaps; but in any case you would not have escaped without, at least, some serious injury or ridiculous scar. But I am mistaken; in you nothing could ever appear ridiculous; you would write a poem on it; a poet can afford to be maimed and resemble Cervantes, or blind—Milton's blindness added much to his fame."

" You are ridiculing me, my dear aunt."

" Because I am so happy to see you with two eyes and both arms.   But, seriously, my dear, we must make that visit to-morrow to Madame de Fleurigny."

This visit, Robert felt, would be a trying ordeal, but he resigned himself to it bravely, wondering all the while if he could with propriety escape it.

Madame de Fleurigny's home at Rillé was most attractive.   The house, built of red brick framed in gray stone, seemed to smile a gracious welcome under its green tile roof.   On the small stream that flowed through the garden a flock of ducks swam in single file; in the tall acacia-trees the pigeons chattered seriously of their affairs, and the church belfry threw its long shadow across the emerald-green sward.   Madame de Fleurigny was busily occupied preparing a baby's basket for a future elector, when the Marquise de Rillé and her nephew, M. de Salemberry, were announced. She rose quickly, contrary to her usually grave manner, and, running to meet the marquise, seized both her hands.

"Oh, my dear friend, your arrival is as timely as Marshal McMahon's at Magenta; I am quite bewildered in the midst of all this lace and trimming, and you will extricate me from my difficulties. Good-morning, M. de Salemberry; you will advise me also. Let us be seated."

"Madame," said Robert, advancing, "I wish to say——"

"That baby-clothes are not easy to make, which I know better than you."

"No, madame; but I do not know how to explain to you——"

"That this cap is too large and this dress too narrow? Say no more; I agree with you. But you, my dear marquise, will understand that it is easy enough to make a large cap smaller; the problem is to increase the width of a narrow dress."

"We shall try to solve it."

"But I see that your nephew is not much interested in the solution. Take a turn in the garden, M. de Salemberry, and if you meet Gilberte let her know that your aunt is here."

Robert went out without having been able to finish his speech. He did not meet Gilberte in the garden, but on looking further he caught sight of her in a little summer-house. The young girl was seated at a rustic wooden table, reading; she seemed deeply absorbed in her book, on the margin of which she from time to time wrote hastily with a gold pencil that glistened in her white fingers. At the sound of Robert's footstep on the gravel, she turned, slightly startled, and, quickly closing her book, extended her hand with prompt cordiality to her visitor. Her eyes had the same mysterious impassibility, but a kind smile played gently on her lips.

Robert, still more embarrassed in the daughter's presence than he had been in her mother's, again attempted the long-prepared speech :

"Mlle. de Fleurigny, I wish to say to you——"

"I, too, have something to say to you, M. de Salemberry."

"I do not know how to explain to you, Mlle. de Fleurigny——"

"Exactly; I also have an explanation to make to you, M. de Salemberry; I shall make mine first, with your permission."

Robert bowed, much astonished and more embarrassed than ever.

"M. de Salemberry, I have a serious reproach to make." Robert trembled.

"Yes, you are more impetuous and imprudent than I could have supposed. Yesterday, for a miserable hare, you abused those poor wretches who intended you no harm."

"What, no harm! But for you, Mlle. de Fleurigny, they would have killed me."

"Not at all, M. de Salemberry; they had no such intention. This is what I want to explain to you: these fearless gypsies wanted to test your courage; they have a mania for frightening people; but they did not succeed with you, and after you left their chief said to me, in his picturesque language: 'Your friend's blood was up, but he kept his head.' The gypsy chief was right; you were in no danger yesterday, but another time your impetuosity may cost you very dear."

"You are generous, Mlle. de Fleurigny, and

I perfectly understand the feeling of delicacy——"

"Delicacy, generosity! I do not understand.
Now let us talk of something else, please."

Robert closed his eyes to keep back the tears
that trembled on the lids.

"Come, let us talk of something else, I beg
of you."

Robert, regaining his self-possession, said:
"I interrupted the reading in which you seemed
so much interested, Mlle. de Fleurigny."

"Yes, M. de Salemberry, very much."

"If I dared—if you would not think me
too indiscreet—I should like to ask what the
book is?"

Gilberte blushed, but made no reply.

"I see I have been very indiscreet; such
familiar curiosity is, I admit, allowable and
pardonable only in a friend."

Gilberte reflected a few moments, then said
suddenly:

"M. de Salemberry, I have no reason to
hide what I do, think, or read. You asked me
what this book is; do you repeat the question?"

" Yes, Mlle. de Fleurigny."

" You really wish to know then? "

" I really do."

" In that case, take and read it."

She handed him the volume, bound in rough leather; Robert opened it and read the title-page: " The Poisonous Fang: A Comedy in Five Acts, by Robert de Salemberry."

" Fate is cruel," murmured Robert, in a hollow voice. He felt the book trembling in his hand, lowered his eyes under Gilberte's searching gaze, and, to cover his increasing embarrassment, he began turning over the leaves.

" Are you looking at the notes written there? " asked Gilberte.

" I dare not allow myself to look at them."

" Why not? You have a great desire to, I imagine."

" That is true."

" Well, then——"

She hesitated a moment.

" Very well, M. de Salemberry; take the book; I give it to you. And now let us join my mother in the drawing-room."

Madame de Rillé was taking leave of her

friend when Gilberte and Robert joined them. As he was leaving them he noticed a portrait on an easel in a corner of the room : one of G. Saint-Pierre's masterpieces. It was difficult to distinguish the picture, almost hidden in shadow, and Robert went towards it to get a better view; but Gilberte, seeing his object, placed herself between him and the portrait.

" No," she said in a low voice; " it is Stephen."

Robert drew back trembling, but made no reply. Gilberte's gaze was no longer cold and impenetrable; subdued lightning flashed from her eyes as they followed Robert's retreating figure.

CHAPTER III.

A YOUNG GIRL'S CRITICISM OF THE COMEDY.

As soon as he was alone in his room, Robert hastened to open the volume Gilberte had given him, feeling more misgiving than on the evening of the first representation of the play. It was not the murmurs of the orchestra, nor the whispers of the parquet that he now had to dread, but the candid judgment of a child.

"Doubtless, she cannot be impartial," he said to himself; "she must defend her brother indignantly and with bitterness against the satirical work. It is very natural that she should look upon me as a monster, and tell me so unsparingly. This promises to be interesting. A young girl's criticism of the theatre—the dove in the rôle of the hawk, cooing ferociously, is quite a new study. I'll submit myself fearlessly to her little claws, for the sake of the amusement it will afford me."

He did well to laugh in anticipation, for what he saw on opening the book was not reassuring. On the first page, the fly-leaf, he found the following:

"I must carefully re-read this comedy, this 'Poisonous Fang,' this abominable attack upon our poor Stephen. My mother weeps every time she speaks of it. Stephen never speaks of it, but I know well that when he is so very sad it is in consequence of this detestable comedy.

"Is it really possible that Robert could have had such a malicious intention? No, no; I cannot believe it; he dearly loved Stephen, who returned his love so generously; and he was always so good to me when I was a little child, and as I grew up.

"Oh! if I could prove that Robert is not to blame, and that my mother, Stephen, and all the others are mistaken. If I could reconcile them, how happy I should be!"

"Poor child! she has courage; why has not her brother?"

At the end of the first scene Gilberte had written;

"How difficult it is to judge; I cannot fail to see how fine, how beautiful all this is; but it seems to me too fine and beautiful. I must be very foolish, for everybody else judges it very differently. The essential point is, that there is, so far, nothing against Stephen; absolutely nothing."

" Beware of what follows," thought Robert, as he resumed the reading of the notes; he found the following on the margin of the fifth scene:

"Ah, here is the poet. This will bear careful examination. It is nothing—he writes verses in an album—that is not a crime, it is merely sentimental; moreover, this poet does not resemble Stephen, who has a horror of such sentimentality. I remember a couplet of his:

" 'On that instrument of torture
Adorned with the name of album.'

This is not Stephen, so far, at least."

"She judges kindly here, but the second act! the second act!"

On the margin of the famous scene of the sonnet, Gilberte's writing had become more nervous, and her comments showed more agitation:

"Yes, yes; this is meant for Stephen — there are words and many things that designate him. This sonnet is evidently a parody on Stephen's sonnets. Let me read further: I must not be too quick to condemn. I must see if there are no excuses, no extenuating circumstances to which Robert might appeal. He certainly was in the wrong—yes, gravely in the wrong—and he feels it, too; for one of the players, to exculpate the author, alludes to *Oronte's* sonnet. I shall read the 'Misanthrope' again to compare it——"

Gilberte's notes stopped here, but were re. sumed on the following page:

"I have read the 'Misanthrope.' I dare not write what I think—all this is too much for a young girl. If I dared, I would confess that, in my opinion, it is not *Oronte* who is ridiculous—it is *Alceste's* peevish humor that makes me laugh. As to the sonnet, I also confess that I do not now find it so ridiculous—it was, no doubt, the way in which it was read at the theatre that made it appear so—I see very well that Molière also intended to ridicule *Oronte*— I am completely bewildered——"

Later on Gilberte had written in very large letters:

"The truth is, if I am not mistaken, comic authors seek everywhere their prey; they live only upon what they kill; and they kill with a sneer. Comedy is by nature decidedly inhuman. If there is any excuse for Robert, it is that he has followed bad example, even at the expense of a friend. However, so far I see nothing abominable, as my mother calls it. There is evidence of fickleness of mind, but not of hardheartedness. I can understand that friendship might resent it, but not die of it; I shall write to Stephen."

"She certainly is an angel of forgiveness," thought Robert.

It seems that the forgiveness, even of an angel, has its limits; for, on the last page of the following act, Gilberte's pencil had written only these words:

"My mother was right; I shall read no more."

The young girl did not keep her word, for at the end of the play Robert found an entire page, written evidently much later than the others:

" I have had a good cry, which has somewhat restored my composure. When the play appeared three years ago, I did not seize all its meaning, or appreciate all its venom—oh, no! I understand now what Stephen must have suffered. And the guilty one, I am sure he ought to have suffered also—like all inhuman beings. I was right—all satirists are inhuman. But I hope they suffer for it. God is just. Who would have believed that Robert would deliberately, coolly, patiently, day by day, write such things as these. He awoke and went to sleep with these thoughts. It is horrible to think of it! My mother and Stephen are too forgiving. I hate him!"

Robert let the book fall.

" She does not know, then, that Stephen was the first offender; I wish she knew it. No, she would not believe me; and why should I cause her another pang? She saved my life, and shall I sadden hers? Never, never!"

Let us leave Robert in the midst of his gloomy reflections, and start for Paris.

CHAPTER IV.

THE CLEVEREST OF PARISIAN ACTRESSES.

This fine eulogy has been deservedly pronounced upon at least a dozen actresses. The one who deserved it most was Maria Orfano, and this compliment was the minimum of the praise bestowed upon her, for as we have already said she was as good as she was intelligent. Her goodness of heart was accompanied by a playful archness, always on the alert.

M. and Mme. de Nolongue brought her, one morning, Robert's letter. She received them cordially, and while reading the letters scanned them both with the corner of her eye. The result of the examination was favorable, for, assuming her most gracious smile, she said:

"Monsieur and madame, I am at your service. This letter of M. de Salemberry's was not at all necessary. What can I do for you?"

"I assure you, madame, the matter is a very delicate one."

"'We love to be flattered for our intelligence.' Do you bring me a sonnet, M. de Nolongue?"

"Fortunately, no, madame; although this is a question of one—the famous sonnet of 'The Poisonous Fang.'"

"Ah, yes; explain, please; let us come to the point."

This "let us come to the point" disconcerted M. de Nolongue, and he found it convenient to throw the burden of explanation on his wife.

"My dear Poncette, explain the affair yourself to Madame Orfano."

"Willingly," replied Poncette.

"Your name is Poncette, madame?"

"But through no fault of mine; it is the Christian name borne by all the women of our family for several generations."

"Parents have singular ideas. Let us proceed."

"This is what brings us to you, madame. You know 'The Poisonous Fang' better than any one else; for our cousin's comedy owes to you——"

"The greatest part of its success—that is agreed. Continue."

"You know this unfortunate play (unfortunate in this sense only) was an attack upon a clever poet——"

"Stephen de Fleurigny. That is, I am indeed sorry to say, true; and I took upon myself to reproach the author for it: which proves that I had courage."

"And a great deal of heart."

"If you wish."

"Then, madame, my husband and I hope to have you as an ally in our project."

"What project?"

"We are fully persuaded that Robert was mistaken, and most unjust, in revenging himself so cruelly on Stephen. We think that the article in *The Viper*, which caused the rupture of their friendship, was not Stephen's, and that he allowed himself, for some unknown reason, to be accused of writing it."

"That is my opinion, also," said the actress, in a grave tone.

" But, madame, our conviction does not suffice," replied Madame de Nolongue. " The
only means of showing Salemberry his mistake
is to discover the real author of the article, and
we have come to Paris for that purpose."

" It certainly was a mistake to name you
Poncette, madame, for you are not descended
from that Pontius Pilate who washed his hands
of innocent blood. What measures do you intend to take to discover this anonymous author?"

" We know none; therefore we rely upon
you to help us."

" Upon me? "

" Yes, on your goodness—your cleverness."

Madame Orfano reflected a moment; then
with a sweet smile, and in her rich, mellow
voice, exclaimed:

" But 'that will require a special scene,' as
said the eminent ——."

" You would do it so well."

" I am not so sure; but, to please you, I shall
try; for you are good people. Let us see.
First of all, have you the article from *The Viper*
with you? "

" No, but I shall send it to you."

"This evening; do not forget."

The beautiful actress again reflected a moment, and then said:

"Do me the honor, M. le Baron, to dine with me next Sunday. I do not invite madame, you understand."

"I accept with great pleasure, madame."

"I shall invite, for the same day, all the editorial staff of *The Viper*, with a few of my other journalist friends, and—and we shall see. Until Sunday, then."

As M. and Mme. de Nolongue were about to take leave, the actress approached him and said, "Baron, come a little nearer the window."

Baron de Nolongue obeyed, and Maria Orfano looked at him a moment, in the strong light:

"I suspected it," pointing to Louis' curled locks; "I thought so. That came from the house of William Thomson, London."

M. de Nolongue blushed crimson.

"I told you so, Louis," said Poncette, excitedly; "it is very evident."

"Madame is right, M. de Nolongue, and because I like you I am going to give you good advice: throw that thing into the fire. You are ungrateful to fate. Just think of it! Nature has done for you what she does for very few people; she has given you the means of appearing grave, serious, profoundly thoughtful, without effort, and you thwart nature. You do not know how many people owe their fortune to the absence of that vain ornament that caused Absalom's death."

Assured by the actress' kindly smile, Louis ventured to say: "My wife is of your opinion, madame, and I should be glad to submit to your and her good judgment, if it were possible."

"Why, is it impossible?"

"Oh, no! But my vanity made me conceal, and I thought I had succeeded in hiding, this— favor of nature; if I were suddenly to make such a public avowal, I should subject myself to retrospective ridicule, for everybody knows that one does not become bald in a single night."

"No," murmured the actress, under her breath, "but sometimes in a single day!"

"What are you saying so softly, madame?"

"That I have found a means of saving the

situation, which will give you confidence in my ability in the affair of *The Viper.*"

"And what is this means, madame?"

"I want to surprise you with it. Read the papers very early to-morrow morning, and act in accordance. Good-by; do not forget my dinner on Sunday, nor the morning papers. You are good people."

M. and Mme. de Nolongue went away very much puzzled. All the next morning's papers contained the following, which evidently had been communicated to them by the Prefecture of Police:

"The fire yesterday in the Faubourg Saint-Antoine gave rise to a most dramatic incident. A six-year-old child had taken refuge on a roof that had just caught fire, when a brave citizen, the Baron de Nolongue, seizing a ladder, rushed to the little one's rescue and carried it through the flames. The child escaped quite scathless; her valiant deliverer was not seriously injured, but his luxuriant hair was entirely consumed as he ran through the flames. The learned Dr. X. declares that the Baron Louis de Nolongue will be bald to the end of his days. The memory of his noble deed will be his best consolation."

Louis de Nolongue and his wife understood the meaning of this article, and he could no longer resist complying with her wishes. Moreover, it brought him good fortune, and, anticipating events, we give here the result of this adventure. The baron's bravery made quite a sensation. A learned man recalled in one of the principal papers the Latin poem written by a monk in honor of Charles the Bald, each word of which began with C:

"Carmina, clarisonæ, clavis cantate, camenæ."

The young baron's heroism made him very popular, and a few months later he was elected deputy from his district. Baron Louis de Nolongue is to-day the handsomest bald-head in the Chamber of Deputies.

CHAPTER V.

Maria Orfano, while awaiting her guests, sat in the large drawing-room of her handsome house in the Rue de la Paix, attentively reading the famous article in *The Viper* that the Baron de Nolongue had sent her. So deeply was she absorbed, she seemed to be learning it by heart.

"I am determined to succeed in this affair. The thing amuses me; it is delightful to punish the author of an evil deed by doing a good one. But I shall find it difficult, for whoever wrote this article ought to be wary of the police, and poachers do not like to let themselves be trapped; but chance aids the vigilant police."

The celebrated actress' guests arrived promptly. As all the others were acquaintances, Maria Orfano had only the Baron Louis de Nolongue to present. Louis was well-known from the account given of the fire in

111

the Faubourg Saint - Antoine, and the late hero's baldness was admired by the fifteen journalists on the faith of the daily papers. Thus is fame acquired-

As this assemblage of fifteen, consisting of journalists, dramatic authors, novelists, and poets sat at table, they, truth to tell, in nowise differed in appearance from a reunion of notaries, brokers, deputies, millionaires, or engineers. The managing editor of *The Viper*, facing the hostess, presided with a dignity the president of the Senate might envy, and the editor of *The Court Calendar* was as solemn as the Procureur-General of the Court of Appeals. It was the fault of the white cravats; the habit makes the monk.

This solemnity did not enter into the actress' plans. After the soup and one or two courses, seeing that her choice Madeira did not succeed in making her guests unbend, she took up the conversation.

"Gentlemen, illustrious representatives of the source of literary news, you think you are, or at least call yourselves, Republicans, but you are in reality the officials of the future monarchy. I have known chamberlains under the Empire less majestic than you. This is anticipating the future too much; take advantage of the Republic while it exists, and be hilarious and triumphant. Are you Republicans? Yes, or no?"

"Yes," answered several voices.

"Then why are you so solemn? Why these prudent glances, these discreet expressions? Are you, perchance, candidates for the French Academy?"

"No, no!" exclaimed all the guests.

"Thank you, gentlemen; I see I have touched a responsive chord. My dear president, call upon one of these orators for a speech."

"I obey, my dear Célimène. I propose that the brilliant writer for *The Viper*, Pierre Robès, give us a speech. Mount the rostrum, my good friend."

"If my chief will give me a subject; I speak or write only under orders."

"Very well; you have just finished a comedy. Tell us of your first appearance on the stage."

"None of that; if the plot of the piece

8

should evaporate, it would make our neighbors sneeze."

" Metaphor aside, you fear the plagiarists ; you flatter yourself, but I understand. Let us try another subject. Why do you call yourself Pierre Robès? That is an uncommon name."

" It is, in fact, a pseudonym."

" And why did you choose it?"

" Because I was refused the baccalaureate degree."

" Tell us about it," said Maria, very graciously.

" It is a melancholy memory, dear madame, but I shall comply with your request in a moment. This salmon-trout will fortify me for the task."

The actress in the meantime carefully studied the young writer. Pierre Robès was a pale, bilious-looking bachelor of thirty ; his hair was thin on brow and temple, his eyes small but full of fire ; he had distended nostrils, and a cynical expression at the corners of his mouth. When he had finished his trout, he continued :

" This is the story, madame. When I was seventeen my father wished me to obtain the degree of bachelor of arts. I presented myself, accordingly, to the Faculty of Paris. I had already a leaning towards literature, but I was as ignorant as that trout before he was caught. However, I did not make such a poor show in Greek and Latin, but I was perfectly at sea in French history, and I floundered shamefully among the Valois. The professor, losing all patience, said: 'Let us see if you can do any better with the French Revolution. Do you know the name of the man who had Danton guillotined?' I had no idea who it was, but the pupil behind me whispered, 'Robespierre.' Not to appear too ignorant, I would not repeat the name just as he whispered it, and I answered, 'Pierre Robès!' A shout of laughter rang through the room, and I was rejected."

"And this gave you the idea of taking——"

"Not so fast. I left France and went everywhere to seek my fortune under my own name. I traversed the shores of Italy, Russia, and America; but the sea is rough, so I returned to France five years ago and plunged into journalism. My father forbade my signing our name to my articles."

" Why ? "

" Provincial prejudice; he feared the family name might be compromised by what I wrote."

" What is this name? "

" Lebon."

" Like the *Sergeant* in 'Tartufe.' "

" You have no idea how near you are to facts; my father is a sergeant."

" Then," said Maria Orfano, laughing, "you are perhaps descended from the *Sergeant* in 'Tartufe' ? "

" That has never been proved. In short, I know not why I took this pseudonym, except that the remembrance of my ignominious failure to obtain a baccalaureate amused me; and now my name is Pierre Robès, and those who think that I do not do credit to it would do well not to say so."

" No one would say it, my dear sir; no one. And the comedy of which we were just now speaking will, no doubt, add new lustre to the name."

" One never knows, madame."

Not wishing to let the conversation flag, she kept up the dialogue with the writer, with her bright eyes all the while steadily fixed upon him.

"Speaking of comedy, M, Pierre Robès, I shall give you a point: Salemberry promises us a new play for next winter."

"The deuce!"

"That annoys you?"

"No, but it makes me anxious for him."

"I do not understand."

"Oh, yes! after the immense success of 'The Poisonous Fang' the public will be very exacting. With all due respect to de Salemberry, were I in his place I should hereafter write only poems, metrical dramas, or tragedies."

"Perhaps you are right. So you admire de Salemberry's poems and dramas very much?"

"I am not afraid of them; I look up to them, but I could no more rise to their height than I could mount the obelisk."

"If the obelisk were to fall, would you be very sorry?"

"I could measure it more conveniently, that is all."

Maria Orfano, feeling that Pierre Robès' inquisition had lasted long enough, turned to the other guests and addressed a few remarks consecutively to each one, thus making the conversation very animated.

At dessert, the actress again addressed the writer:

"You do not take fruit, M. Robès? You make a mistake—'*The duchess' pears are not the least tender!*'"

And she emphasized the phrase with her loveliest smile.

"Where have I read that phrase?" asked the journalist in reply. "Ah, yes, I remember; in an article in *The Viper*, four years ago. It made sensation enough, did that same article."

"Yes, indeed, and I have never been able to discover the author," said the director of *The Viper*. "The reader, short of copy, took it at random from the box of manuscript and printed it to fill a space. No, I am mistaken; he found it on the form, all printed. But no one ever knew who gave it to the compositor. I remember, now, charging Pierre Robès, who had just taken a place on the paper, to inquire into the subject; do you remember it, Robès?"

"Perfectly; but all my efforts were in vain."

"You are acting very shrewdly, my dear M. Robes," said the actress, rising.

As they entered the drawing-room, where coffee was served, Maria Orfano made a sign to Baron Louis de Nolongue, drew him a little aside, and, glancing toward Pierre Robès, said:

"There is the author of the article."

"Is it possible? How have you made——"

"Nothing simpler; I made him talk a great deal, as you may have noticed. I am accustomed to commit parts to memory, so I learned this famous article almost by heart, you see. Then I have been much in the society of journalists and writers, and I long ago observed that they speak very much as they write. The construction of the phrase is the same; the source of ideas, opinions, and sentiments is the same. My suspicions were aroused by M. Robes' first words, and that remark about the obelisk convinced me without anything else. That is all for the present; 'continued in our next number.'"

The actress approached Pierre Robès and said:

"Your story interests me deeply, my dear M. Robès, and I should like to be of service to you."

"Madame," said the journalist, all smiles and bowing profoundly.

"For what theatre is your comedy intended?"

"I should like to offer it to Jacques Alençon——"

"My manager?"

"Yes, but I do not know him, and you know——"

"I shall give you a letter; you will send it to him to-morrow with your manuscript, and you will go to see him the next day at noon. Do not forget."

"I shall be very sure to be there on time."

"Is there a part for me in your play?"

"Oh, yes."

"That may serve to influence Jacques' decision. But I must warn you that he is not a man easy to manage. You must do everything he may ask you—that is, if you are desirous of having your play acted."

"Desirous! as I am of retaining life."

"Good; I see you have no taste for suicide;

so much the better. I pledge myself to see this through."

The charming woman, looking after Robès as he left, said to herself, smiling with inward joy:

"I was not sure that the scene could be made,—but it is made."

CHAPTER VI.

A THEATRICAL MANAGER'S RUSE.

JACQUES ALENCON received Maria Orfano in his private office; at five minutes to twelve she arose to take leave of her manager.

"Well, you promise me to do all that, my dear manager?"

"Yes, my charming star; I like to serve good people."

"'Being one myself,' you might add, as in 'The King Amuses Himself.' You, at least, understand perfectly?"

"That is a courteous question."

"I mean, do you remember all the points?"

"Yes, oh, yes! Stephen—Salemberry—the mother, the sister—the husband with the wig —*The Viper*—the journalist. What an excellent title for a fable: 'The Viper and the Journalist'!"

"Do not jest, but attend to our affairs; you promise me again——"

"You distrust me?"

"Always."

"In this instance you will be mistaken."

"It is twelve. I escape by the door to the left; our man enters by the door on the right. You remain standing in the middle of the room in front of the fireplace. Very good stage-setting. *Au revoir,*" she called back, disappearing at left, as she said.

Jacques Alençon was a refined, handsome, distinguished-looking man of about sixty, charming as a man of the world, but fierce as a manager. His ferocity, however, was only a mask which he assumed at will when it was necessary; he could with equal facility assume the mask of amiability, as well as that of impassiveness.

He chose the latter in which to receive Pierre Robès.

"Be seated, sir, and let us discuss this matter seriously. What do you think of your play?"

"What do I think of my play? But it seems to me that it is you who——"

"You are mistaken, sir; I think it very important to know an author's opinion of his work; when I may believe, *a priori*, that he is a writer of considerable merit."

"Really, sir, I think if you had found it very bad you would have told me so at once."

"I do not decide things so quickly.   No, M. Robès, a piece may not be bad, yet despite that it may not be good.   These very cases are the most troublesome to a manager."

"Is this the case with my comedy?"

"I admit that it is not bad, and at times I am inclined to think, too, that perhaps it is rather good."

"Then you will have it played?"

"Your piece, as it is now, would be a good deal of an undertaking,—quite a troublesome affair."

"It is only three short acts!"

"There are no short acts; in fact, all three are twice too long."

"It is not bad to have abundant material."

"When the material is solid."

"Is mine?"

"Things are tested by use."

"Finally, sir, do you intend to have my piece played?"

"I do, and I do not; it may be, and it may not be played."

"What a sphinx you are!"

"That is my profession."

"In short, what do we decide?"

"That you will reduce your work to half its present dimensions; that done, you will bring it to me."

"I understand, and I thank you, for you seem to be interested in me."

"Am I wrong?"

"No, I am not a bad sort of a devil, after all."

"Then you may be made an angel."

"With difficulty. I am a queer body."

"A queer body—who has many skeletons."

"They are well buried; that is enough," replied Pierre Robès, laughing. As he rose to leave, Jacques Alençon accompanied him to the door, and, scrutinizing him closely with his penetrating eye, said, in a serious tone:

"By the way, M. Robès, I have a favor to ask of you."

"Speak, prince; your highness——"

"My highness, for very particular reasons, wishes to know the author of an unsigned article."

"That may be ascertained. What day did the article appear?"

"Four years ago."

"The deuce! And in what paper?"

"In *The Viper.*"

"We are getting warm. The subject of the article?"

"A rather disparaging depreciation of Robert de Salemberry's works."

"Ah, yes; I know the article."

"It is the name of the author that I want to know."

"What for?"

"To tell it to M. de Salemberry, and thus prove that he made a mistake in attacking such a good, loyal fellow as Stephen de Fleurigny."

Pierre Robès was silent a moment, then said:

"If I succeed in discovering the name you are seeking, I should much prefer to tell it to Salemberry myself."

"There is no objection to that. When you

have discovered it you will write and tell it to Salemberry."

" And then? "

" Then, you will bring me Robert de Salemberry's answer, and at the same time your revised comedy."

" And you will then decide in favor of my comedy? "

" Probably."

" *Au revoir*, then; I go to commence my search."

" Do not unearth too many skeletons, young man; one will be sufficient for me, but soon."

Pierre Robès went away quite perplexed, thoughtfully murmuring to himself:

" A sword-thrust is a very disagreeable thing—granted; but it is a very gratifying thing to have a grand piece played. It will be difficult to cope with these good little comrades. This Jacques Alençon is a sly dog; what a minister of foreign affairs he would make; I am determined to fathom this idea. And Maria Orfano, what an artful creature—no matter. But this prospective sword-thrust—bah! "

When Robès reached his modest apartment,

he sharpened his finest quill, and in a firm hand
wrote the following letter to Robert de Salemberry :

" *Illustrious Master.*

"Sɪʀ :—I am about to render you a service
at my own risk and peril.   For reasons entirely
personal, I have been most anxious to discover
the author of an article that appeared several
years ago in *The Viper,* in which your talents and
character were not treated with the deference
they deserve.   I have succeeded in this quest.

"The author in question is one of my most
intimate friends.   You may not have forgotten
the journey and visit you made to Florence
about five years ago, where you received a most
flattering reception from the Duke and Duchess
of X.   Well, my friend had some cause of
complaint against the duke, but especially
against the duchess.   With your leave, I shall
not press this point.

"My friend, whom you do not know, and
who, moreover, has, since then, changed his
name, conceived a feeling of hatred for you,
that I do not attempt to justify.   The desire

to revenge himself was the motive that impelled him to commit this injustice; hence this deplorable article, for which he now blushes, and that double-meaning phrase, '*the duchess' pears,*' which was meant to wound you by wounding another.

"This was not the only wrong my friend perpetrated. Public rumor accused M. Stephen de Fleurigny of having written this doubly culpable article. My friend did nothing to contradict this false accusation—perhaps even helped to spread it.

"In now making this tardy acknowledgment of his long-concealed double offence, my friend understands that he must accept the consequences.

"Unfortunately, his state of health will not permit him to fight a duel, but I have decided to be his substitute, and I am at your disposition.

"Assuming, then, that the offender is none other than Pierre Robès,

"Accept, illustrious sir, etc.,

"PIERRE ROBES,

"Editor of *The Viper.*"

9

Two days later, Pierre Robès received the following reply:

"SIR:—The service you have rendered me in showing me the truth makes me forget all else. I must decline your offer to act as substitute for your friend; if he ends better than he began, he will have a narrow escape.

"Believe me, sir, with the very divers sentiments with which you inspire me,

"ROBERT DE SALEMBERRY."

Pierre Robès showed this letter to Jacques Alençon. The manager and the actress kept their promise, the writer's piece was played, and had even a certain amount of success. Literary success is sometimes blind, like victory and military fame.

CHAPTER VII.

THE REAL VICTIM.

I⊤ would be difficult to depict Robert de Salemberry's overwhelming despair. Every word of Pierre Robès' letter went to his heart like a knife.

Let us not make our hero seem better than he was; his pride was what suffered most in this affair.

"Well, I was deceived; I made a serious mistake in laying the offence to the charge of one who was not at all to blame. My logic misled me into striking a false blow. My judgment was at fault and swerved from the path of justice. I knew not why Stephen refused to defend himself, but I ought to have guessed. Believing that I was punishing treachery, I committed a great wrong. There are two men in the world who knew it. Stephen may despise me, Pierre Robès must laugh; he has made me a laughing-stock. He is the wretch who made me rush into this attack upon an innocent man. Hercules wages war on a pigmy; it has been a very stupid affair. Why are such things permitted? Sagacity and infallibility should always accompany ability and intelligence. What am I to do now? What can I do? My aunt builded better than she thought with her 'Game of Virtues': 'Repair the injury that has been done.' One might believe that she had prescience. It is strange that she, as well as M. and Mme. de Nolongue and Maria Orfano in Paris, everybody in fact, judged more justly than I. It is humiliating. Of what avail are talents, knowledge of the human heart, reputation, fame? Oh, that dreadful comedy! that hideous title, ' The Poisonous Fang,' that I thought so much of, and considered so good! What misery it all is now!"

Robert, finding at hand a copy of his play, shuddered at sight of it and threw the book aside.

" I cannot remain quiet with these thoughts; I must act. First, I shall go find my aunt; she will give me good advice."

Robert hurried down from his room in the castle tower, but was told that Madame de Rillé had just gone to pay a visit to Mme. and Mlle. de Fleurigny.

"With Stephen's mother and sister. I should have been there long ago."

"What is the matter, my illustrious nephew?" exclaimed the marquise, as Robert entered Madame de Fleurigny's drawing-room. "Have you had another fight with the gypsies? You are as pale——"

"Mlle. de Fleurigny," said Robert, "will you kindly read this letter to these ladies? I have not the courage to do it myself."

Gilberte read Pierre Robès' letter slowly, in a tremulous voice in which joy and surprise were mingled.

A prolonged silence followed the reading of the letter, during which Robert waited with downcast eyes; no one dared utter a word.

Finally, the Marquise de Rillé said:

"Nephew, I ask pardon for you from Madame de Fleurigny, her daughter, and from her absent son, Stephen. As for you, be your own judge."

"I have already judged and condemned myself, aunt."

"That is not enough; you must now repair the injury you inflicted."

"I am ready to do all in my power."

"What do you intend to do?"

"First, I shall write to the papers; publicly acknowledge that I was mistaken, and that I attacked the best and noblest of friends."

"Pardon me, M. de Salemberry," interrupted Gilberte, "but that would be publishing that the odiously ridiculous character placed by you upon the stage was really intended to represent Stephen. That would only establish the fact and aggravate the injury."

"That is true, Mlle. de Fleurigny; what can I do then?"

"Nothing, sir."

"You are mistaken, my child; if M. de Salemberry has no objection, that letter, at least, might be sent to Stephen."

"I was going to beg you to do so, madame; only allow me to add a line to the letter."

Robert, taking a pen from the table, wrote

at the end of the last page: "Will you ever forgive me, Stephen?"

"Very well, M. de Salemberry; I shall write to my son."

"While you are writing, mother, allow me a few moments' private conversation with M. Robert."

"Do as you wish, my child; you are always right."

Gilberte led Robert to her favorite summer-house in the garden.

"You must know all, M. de Salemberry, but I have no right to speak before your aunt of a secret known only to my mother, Stephen, and to me." The young girl hesitated an instant, the habitual, fixed expression of her eyes was replaced by a sudden flash, and she continued in a trembling voice:

"You think, no doubt, M. de Salemberry, that your attack upon Stephen merely wounded his self-love, and lessened his reputation as a poet; that would have been nothing, for, after all, these things retrieve themselves and are soon forgotten. You inflicted a much more ir-reparable injury upon my brother. He loved,

and was to marry a young lady, Isabelle d'Acérac,
daughter of the general.   When your piece was
played, her father went to Stephen and insisted
upon his challenging you, which my brother refused to do; and yet you know how brave Stephen is; but you know how good he is also, and
that he does not agree with the world on certain subjects.   He is a saint!   The engagement
was broken and Isabelle married another."

"Oh, just Heaven!" exclaimed Robert; "if
I had known."

Tears welled to the young man's eyes.

"It astonishes me to see tears in your eyes,
sir; I considered you hard-hearted—yes, very
hard-hearted.   I have seen my dear, noble
brother weep before I saw your tears.   He
would not add to my mother's suffering by
grieving before her, but he told me of his tender love for Isabelle, and his sobs and despair-
ing anguish broke my heart.   Ah! may you
suffer thus some day, for you deserve it.   And
while he wept, you were enjoying your horrible triumph, listening to the public sneers and
laughter; hearing the noble name of your friend
vilified, bandied from mouth to mouth, and

those malicious people calling him 'that poor
Stephen.' This was pleasant to you, and you
had even a baser gratification from it; you made
money by your perfidious, vindictive work; yes,
in the evening you counted your money, the
gold and the bank-notes the cashier brought
you from the theatre, and said, 'This is good;
friends are lucrative.'"

"Oh, Mlle. de Fleurigny!" exclaimed Robert, pale with emotion.

"What I say wounds you; so much the better. I am not gentle and ready to forgive, like
my brother. No; in his place I should have
done as the general wished. I should have
challenged you—I should have killed you—I
should have silenced your ironical, disdainful
lips forever. And the other day, in the woods,
when those men were about to pound you to
death with their stones, hatchets, and hammers,
I was on the point of letting them do it. I did
save you; I told you that I did not, but it is
true—I saved you. Why? I know not, except it seemed to me that Stephen was there
and called to me, 'Save him! save him!' But
I cannot always be generous like him; I have

all this in my heart, and I must cast it in your face.   Now, go; before the world, I shall behave towards you as a well-bred young girl should towards a clever man; but you know how I feel at heart.   Good-morning, sir; leave me."

"Mlle. de Fleurigny, you are more cruel than I have been," replied Robert, as he turned to go.

That same evening Gilberte received an envelope bearing the stamp of the Bureau for the Relief of the Poor, and containing a copy of a paper on file at that office:

"Received of M. de Salemberry the sum of 110,000 francs, the entire receipts from his rights in the comedy, 'The Poisonous Fang.' According to the intention of the donor, this sum will be distributed among the poor of Paris.

"COMMISSIONER OF PUBLIC RELIEF.
"PARIS, December 8, 1875."

The date of this receipt coincided with the last representation of "The Poisonous Fang," three years before.

"Ah," thought Gilberte, "I, too, have been hard and unjust, but in this only."

The hardness and injustice of which Gilberte accused herself was of benefit to Robert in his present state of mind. What he took most to heart, what completely overwhelmed him, was the dreadful reproach of having gained money, acquired fortune, filled his coffers with the profits of his iniquitous work. Nothing helps us to comprehend the wrong we do others like a similar wrong done to us. The shock, while wounding us, teaches us in return a useful lesson.

"I appreciate now what Stephen must have suffered when I accused him to his face so cruelly and unjustly. I understand how it was that he could not defend himself; I could find no answer to Gilberte's bitter reproaches yesterday, and if I had not found the proof of my innocence on that point she would still believe that I had Judas' thirty pieces of silver in my pocket. Her reproaches, nevertheless, came home to me, went straight to my heart, and cut me to the quick. Ah, poor Stephen! my poor Stephen! And that young girl whom he loved, from whom he was separated by my criminal deed—for it was a crime before God. What agony he must have endured! It seems to me

that I can see and hear him when he contem-
plated, in mournful despair, his dream of happiness fading away forever.   Oh, how gladly I
would give my fame, my fortune, and my life
to redeem one of those tears.   I recall now all
our friendship, the care he took of my growing
reputation, his loving, earnest counsel.   And
his cry at Mars-la-Tour, when he threw himself
between me and that Uhlan's sword—'It might
better be I ; you have genius.'   It did not, however, prevent his piercing the Uhlan's head with
a ball from his revolver.   And I forgot all that,
and yielded to a vile suspicion, to newspaper
and drawing-room gossip, and made this hero,
this friend weep like a child.   Oh, stupid, vil-
lainous pride, well might I blush for it !   Poor
Stephen, what will he say when he receives this
letter ?   If the wound has healed it will reopen,
and he will curse me again, and justly."

Stephen's answer came promptly :

"ROME, October 25, 1879.
"MY DEAR ROBERT :
"I forgave you long ago, or, rather, I have
never blamed any one but myself for your mis-

take. Through a feeling of excessive dignity I would not defend myself against your accusation; I was wrong, hence came all the trouble. Do not further reproach yourself; I shall tell you some day, soon I hope, how you have been the maker of my future happiness. I received with yours a letter from my dear Gilberte. It seems to me that the scene she made with you was rather too theatrical for a young girl. I shall scold her for it.

"On your part, do not hold this too much against her. I have always dreaded this meeting for you both. You have no sister, and you do not know how tenderly these little souls love their big brothers. I know one in the highest social circles, who made a vow to enter a convent if her elder brother returned from the war; she is now a Carmelite.

"Gilberte will never become a Carmelite, but you have had sufficient proof that she does not lack strength of character. Console yourself by saying, 'I have seen the wrath of the Lamb,' as the Scripture says.* I shall not finish my

* "Abscondite nos a facie sedentis super thronum et ab ira Agni."—*Apocalypse, vi. 16.*

letter without reproaching you very seriously.
You no longer work, you are doing nothing.
Why?

"I can guess why, my dear Robert, or rather
I am quite sure I know. You no longer do
anything because your last work turned you
from your true course, from your natural bent.
You were not made for this jeering, satirical
rôle. The success you achieved is your punish-
ment. You were the lion who went to the
monkeys in the mountain, and on returning the
'large-headed seigneur' made grimaces at the
passers-by; a very bad habit, and difficult to
correct. What a pity! he was so noble, proud,
and handsome! This is why I seek a quarrel
with the lion. You will become again that lion
that I loved, and shall always love, my dear
Robert; it is your duty. I knew you to have the
highest ambition, the ambition to give to France
works elevating to mind and soul, of which she
has so much need. You have labored to amuse
the Philistines; work rather to create the great
and powerful, and to win their applause. Yes,
my dear friend, work for France, give her sublime intellectual food; should she disdain it, it

will not be your fault, and she will return to it sooner or later.

"I impose upon you as a penance to arouse your genius, and I say to you as the Master said to Peter: '*Duc in altum!*' *

"I have finished my little sermon, dear Robert; be thankful that I did not put it into a sonnet, at which you would be inclined to laugh. Forgive this little piece of mischievous pleasantry, which is only a playful evidence of my friendship for you.

"With a loving embrace,

"STEPHEN DE FLEURIGNY."

Robert involuntarily pressed Stephen's letter to his lips. " Yes, I will do your bidding, your wish shall be mine; I will be what I ought to be, and I shall owe it all to you. Oh! what a noble, generous heart; how readily he forgets, how well he knows how to comfort! But I will not forget, I will never forget; my irreparable mistake will be ever before my eyes and my heart will always be tortured with bitter, undying remorse. I am the real victim myself."

* Launch out into the deep.

CHAPTER VIII.

THE CID'S ERROR.

ROBERT did not see Gilberte again for several days. The fever of work had again seized him, and he shut himself up in his turret-room, coming down only to join his aunt at table, when he chatted a few moments with her, then returned to renew his work.

One day after breakfast he said quite joyfully to the good marquise; "I have finished the first act; I shall read it to you if you wish."

"What first act?"

"The first act of my drama."

"What drama?"

"The Cid's Error."

"What is 'The Cid's Error?'"

"You will see."

"Let us see, then, at once."

Although the marquise often chided her nephew, she was very proud of him, and her

self-love was flattered when Robert made her
the confidant of his labors.

" Go, get us your manuscript and let us
begin."

Robert complied, but just as he began to
read, Mme. and Mlle. de Fleurigny were announced.

" You come very opportunely, my dear
friends. Robert is going to read me the first
act of his new work. Stay, and we three shall
form a small tribunal, enthusiastic, if there is
occasion, but very severe if necessary."

" You do us too much honor," said Madame
de Fleurigny, not without a slight touch of
bitterness.

" Since chance seems to favor my secret desire," interrupted Robert, " I earnestly pray you
to be good enough to listen to this new work.
I assure you the honor is to me alone."

" What do you think, Gilberte ? "

Gilberte turned upon Robert that sphinx-like
gaze of which we have already spoken, and said
deliberately :

" Let us stay, mother."

Robert began to read. The plot of his drama

10

was very simple. The Cid in his youth was
chosen to arbitrate in a quarrel between two
kings. He had cause of complaint against one
of them, the memory of which so influenced his
judgment that, notwithstanding his great equity,
he condemned the king whom he believed to
have wronged him. The king thus condemned,
despoiled of his kingdom, died in exile. Meantime, the son of the vanquished prince pro-
claimed, and offered to prove, his father's innocence. At the end of the first act of the
drama, he came to ask the Cid to revoke the
unjust edict. The Cid, after mature reflection,
acknowledges his error and pledges himself to
repair it. The allusions were very transparent;
the Cid was de Salemberry himself; and it was
very evident that the unjustly condemned king
was Stephen. Robert's three auditors recognized them at once, and their interest was intensely excited from the first moment.

The poet read with extraordinary power and
fervor. His voice gave the resonance of a
clarion to the verses, which were superb in
their movement, like the noble bearing of the
herald-at-arms who, in olden times, announced

the opening of the lists. Familiar scenes, at times almost comic, were introduced with dramatic effect. Robert had discovered the point at which the sublime and the familiar meet, which is the dream, the ambition, and often the despair of writers. The work was, consequently, vigorously bold, strong, and incisive. The young prince's plaint before the Cid, as well as the Cid's monologue, drew silent tears from the women's eyes.

As the reading ended the marquise exclaimed:

"I recognize in this my noble Robert. I am no judge of these things, but I appreciate their beauty; tears are an unmistakable tribute to excellence."

"That is very true, my dear," added Madame de Fleurigny; "my heart thrilled through it all."

"And you, Mlle. de Fleurigny?" ventured Robert.

"Oh, sir, I shall be more severe, perhaps. I shall tell you what I think on our way to the village."

"I submit to your judgment in advance."

"That is a mistake, M. de Salemberry. I am sincere, but not infallible."

The three ladies, accompanied by Robert, walked along the road to Rillé, the mother and the aunt a little in advance. Gilberte, deep in thought, seemed scarcely conscious of Robert's presence at her side.

"Well, Mlle. de Fleurigny, the culprit awaits his sentence."

Gilberte blushed slightly, and, with apparent effort rousing herself from her long revery, said :

"I made a very imprudent promise. I am only a young girl, little versed in the great questions of art and literature; my opinion has no value except to myself. I feel also that it is very easy to misjudge, and then——"

She stopped suddenly, lightly touching the branch of a tree with the end of her parasol.

"And then—— You are laughing at me."

"Laughing at you, Mlle. de Fleurigny! I laugh at you! You know too well that could not be."

"Well," continued Gilberte earnestly, "not-

withstanding my ignorance, incompetence, if
you like it better—I have a passion for literature; I adore Corneille."

And she added, smiling:

"Like a princess of the Fronde, while listening to you I naturally thought of my old friend
Corneille, and I said to myself as you were
reading that first act, how would Corneille have
rendered such a scene? That was very preten-
tious, was it not?"

"No, but it is very flattering to me to be
compared to Corneille."

"Precisely. I compared the young prince's
plaint, which I confess brought tears to my
eyes, to the plaints and sorrows of Chimène;
and I said to myself, pardon my presumption,
that your drama would be much more touching
if, instead of a son, you had given a daughter to
the king unjustly condemned by the Cid."

"Why so, Mlle. de Fleurigny?"

"Because a son could revenge himself, and a
daughter could only make plaint."

"I admit that; I agree with you."

"Then this young man, this soldier, would
necessarily co-operate with the Cid in the

reparation of his error . . . and I should rather
that the Cid would bear the entire burden."

"That is very true, very just. You are perfectly right. Why did I not think of this?
The king shall have a daughter, that is decided.
However, wait. I shall leave him a son also,
a brother and sister. The sister will love her
brother as——"

"If you wish, M. de Salemberry," replied
Gilberte impetuously.

"I beg of you not to hesitate if you have any
further criticism to make, for you will be doing
me a great service."

"Really? Well, then, I think that the Cid
allowed himself to be very easily deceived."

"Oh, I do not believe that, Mlle. de Fleurigny."

"Then I shall not insist upon it; you have,
doubtless, your own reasons."

"Is that meant to be epigrammatic?"

"No, something better."

"Continue, please. I see you still have
something to reprehend."

"Yes, M. de Salemberry, but I dare not say
more."

"Do, I beg of you."

"Well, then, it seems to me that the Cid did not recognize his error soon enough; he resisted the light, and there was too much humiliated pride in his chagrin; if he does not deplore his error with adequate bitterness, he will not make sufficient reparation."

"I yield this point. I shall modify the monologue. Is that all?"

"That is all."

"I thank you from the depths of my heart, Mlle. de Fleurigny. But how did you acquire such penetration, such a rare sense of justice, and such quick, unerring judgment?"

"I do not possess all these qualities, M. de Salemberry, but if I did I should owe them to my favorite poet, who is, as I have told you, Corneille, and after Corneille——"

At this moment they were just entering the drawing-room of the little house at Rillé; Gilberte led Robert to her brother's portrait, and, standing in front of it, finished her sentence:

"After Corneille, to Stephen."

"I saw that at once; while listening to you I almost thought it was he that was speaking."

Gilberte, whose eyes suddenly assumed their mysterious gravity, added in a low voice:

"The other day, when you wished to look at this portrait, I prevented you, rather bruskly, if I remember. Now, I permit you to look at Stephen," she said gravely, as she walked slowly away.

When taking his leave, Robert said to her, almost beseechingly:

" You have been generously kind and helpful to me, Mlle. de Fleurigny; will you not continue your goodness and allow me, while pursuing my labors, to claim for my work your advice, just as you have given it to-day?"

Gilberte turned her gaze upon Stephen's portrait,—then, looking at Robert, said:

"Yes, M. de Salemberry."

Robert, usually so ready to chat with his aunt, did not address a word to her on the way from the village to the castle. The good marquise noticed this, but respected his revery, and when they reached home said to him, smiling:

"Yes, Robert, I am of your opinion."

"The Cid's Error" progressed rapidly after this excellent beginning. Robert set to work again and gave himself up to it with a sort of desperation, and with a feeling of satisfaction that he had not experienced for a long time. Every week he assembled his small audience and read to them what he had written. The marquise and Mme. de Fleurigny were content to admire, but Gilberte continued her rôle of censor and adviser.

A noble woman displays in her judgment of intellectual works the same tact she shows in her intercourse with the world; she quickly recoils from all that shocks her delicacy and rectitude; her instinct warns her even before her reason; her purity loves and seeks that which it resembles, and she guides herself in the serene heights of thought like the swan over the azure depths.

Such a woman was Gilberte. In this inter-change of ideas, she, as well as Robert, gained much. He acquired greater accuracy, and more sustained loftiness of sentiment and ex-pression. She was brought in touch with the noblest problems of the human heart, enjoyed the exquisite pleasure of watching the budding and growth of a new work, and of contemplating

poetry all aglow in its descent from regions to
which the vulgar never attain.

Gilberte one day received a letter from her
brother, of which the following are a few
extracts :

"DEAR, PRECIOUS SISTER:

"What you tell me about 'The Cid's Error'
interests me intensely.   Robert is here on his
own ground, and if he fails it will be at least a
noble ruin.   Whatever the success may be, his
mind and soul will be again attuned to higher
things; all else is of little importance.

"So you give him advice, my little Sévigné,
and you want to know if I approve.   Certainly.
If my formidable friend seeks to repair the injury he has done, let us aid him in his efforts,
that he may be spared any unexpected suffering,
for you see that when a fault is not repaired it
must be expiated.

"This is the general idea of his drama (I was
going to say of *your* drama), if I have understood it aright.   However, he should not insist
too much upon the expiation imposed upon the
Cid; he is so exalted a character in history

and legend, it would be wrong to disparage him.

"Think over this, for I have misgivings about it; but Robert will carry away my doubts in the lion's skin. . . .

"What you add about his receipts as author of 'The Poisonous Fang' having been given to the poor gives me pleasure. You ask if you ought to apologize for the unjust reproaches you made him on this subject. I do not think it necessary—he understands you.

"You would like very much to know what I am doing in Rome, and why I remain here so long. This is still a secret, but in a little while you will know all, and you, as well as mother, will be very happy.

"*Adieu*, till we meet again, my good, noble Gilberte. I hold you and mother to my heart, once so severely wounded, but now completely healed.   STEPHEN."

"The Cid's Error" was finished in two months, and Robert started for Paris, where the rehearsals were soon to begin. Madame de Rillé promised to be present at the first representation, to which she looked forward with great pleasure.

"If I dared, Mlle. Gilberte," said Robert, "I should ask you to come to see my play."

"Perhaps I may, M. de Salemberry; I shall consult Stephen."

CHAPTER IX.

A MANAGER ON HOT COALS.

THERE are always people to be found willing to fill the most dangerous and laborious positions; to be bailiffs, policemen, physicians, firemen on locomotives, ministers of finance, to make ascensions in balloons, to venture into private drawing-rooms, to listen to Wagner's operas. There are those who will enter the tiger's cage and even the lion's den. These last are the theatrical managers, the most heroic of all.

A theatrical manager is a tyrant and a slave; he preys upon others and is preyed upon in turn; he is obliged to wage furious war with actors and actresses, scene-shifters, machinists, decorators, prompters, newspaper-men, subscribers, with the public, but above all with the authors. He can scarcely be said to live by this terrible way of practising his profession, yet if he did not carry it on in this manner it would be the death of him.

Jacques Alençon was the most courageous and the most unfortunate of these voluntary martyrs. The setting of each new piece was an incessant and complicated torture to him. Nevertheless, he threw himself body and soul into the work, with an apparent composure which increased his inward suffering. His trouble began with the necessity of judging the piece itself; he had knowledge, experience, and quick perception, but these three excellent qualities only added to his natural and acquired perplexity, making him see and feel all the defects, which he carefully weighed and balanced with the good qualities. This is the delicate, cruel operation, the refinement of petty injustice that theatrical managers have to endure: The prologue is not clear; the second scene but a repetition of the first; there is a story that may create a laugh, but the effect of the last scene is grand—perhaps—for nothing is certain. Then the struggle with the actors to obtain from them, by flattering their self-love, the best their talent is capable of, adroitly suggesting what they should do, while seeming to let them have the merit of it; saying to them, for example: "It seemed to me yesterday that you were remarkably graceful and your intonation was excellent," which was nothing less than the truth.   Finally, the difficulty of preventing one from producing an effect at the expense of another, "from drawing the covering away from her," as they say in theatrical slang.   These are not trifling difficulties, and even a diplomatic manager finds it no easy task always to overcome them.

Jacques Alençon possessed this great art, but he paid dearly for it.   What he really enjoyed was planning and setting the scenes, arranging the groups to form beautiful tableaux, superintending the designing of the costumes to make them harmonize.   He was perfect master of this secondary but most important part of a very special science.

After these efforts and long struggles, accompanied by feverish activity and insomnia, he finds himself face to face with the unknown —with an *alea*, chance; for success or failure hangs upon a trifle.

Such were Jacques Alençon's thoughts the morning of the first representation of "The Cid's Error," which he thoroughly appreciated and even admired, as much as a manager may seem to admire. But he would have tossed up on its success. His anxiety, however, betrayed itself in spite of him, and before the curtain rose he walked about the stage as if treading on hot coals.

As to Robert de Salemberry, despite a certain feeling of interest, he was calm and confident. Seated in a proscenium box behind Mesdames de Rillé and de Fleurigny and Mlle. Gilberte, he heard the signal for the raising of the curtain with less fear than curiosity, as if he were about to witness and judge the work of another.

The audience seemed unusually eager. The evening of a first representation the author calculates upon a dozen devoted friends convinced of his talent, and twelve hundred secret or avowed enemies. After the pronounced and prolonged success of "The Poisonous Fang," it was very natural that the public should be on the alert, and, if they had not expressly determined to destroy their recent idol, they would reflect before putting him on a higher pedestal.

The first scene of "The Cid's Error" produced a grand effect; the brilliant, sonorous verses were received with great applause. The second scene, which was piquantly comic, delighted the audience; the rôle of the cowardly, famished valet caused frank shouts of laughter; it was too successful. The following scene, which was purely tragic, was not understood. The audience had taken a false scent, and they missed the gayety of the preceding scene. The entrance of the Cid failed in effect; the simple, familiar language in which the poet clothed his speech bewildered the spectators, who supposed that this also was a comic rôle; and when the grand old Campeador expressed himself in nobler language they were surprised and disconcerted. Nevertheless, the end of this first act, full of fervor and beauty, was vigorously applauded. Success was possible.

Robert went behind the curtain, where he met the manager, who stood nervously tapping with his cane on the rests of the stage scenery.

11

" Are you satisfied? " asked the poet.

" I shall answer you after the last act."

" But it really seems to me——"

" Yes, yes; but the shark does not seem much inclined to nibble at the bait."

" It will nibble at it in the second act."

" Provided it does not upset the boat."

" We have safety-buoys."

" A pitiful resource in a stormy sea."

In the actors' gallery Robert was surrounded by a crowd of the three kinds of friends described by the morose philosopher: those who love, those who do not love, and those who hate. They congratulated him, pressed his hand, and embraced him, but the friends of the third category did not seem disturbed.

One of them said to his companion as they went out:

" We did well to congratulate him after the first act."

" You fear, then, that the others——"

" My dear, when one is in the house he feels very quickly if it is likely to fall."

" You make me fear for our poor friend."

" Fraud ! "

"You saw the rehearsal as well as I; do you think that the second act may be hissed?"

"Gourmand!"

It was not hissed; on the contrary, one magnificent scene created a sort of enthusiasm, but the rest was coldly received. There was applause also when the curtain fell.

"Well?" said the man who had just been speaking to his companion.

"Well, he has exhausted his stock of the sublime."

The effect of the third act was mournful. It was evident that the crowd did not grasp the poet's meaning. A few brilliant passages relieved the torpor, but the piece was condemned.

"There is no more danger," said the amiable *confrère* of whom we have already spoken, "there is no more danger, we may applaud"; and he raised his hands while applauding, that Robert might see him.

In the public corridor an epigram, something like this, was circulated, the author of which was unknown:

" Unjust throughout the drama is.   To earn his daily bread
   The prince becomes a pencil-peddler in the play ;
   His daughter loses heaven, as the author lost his head ;
   And the chief fault of the Cid is that the public has to pay."

The last two acts were listened to with pity.
No one hissed, for great talent always commands respect, but a gentle drowsiness reigned
from the orchestra to the front boxes; the fair
spectators showed all their pearly teeth between
their rosy lips, but not in smiles.   The author's
name was mentioned in the midst of the *cla-
queurs'* applause, the actors were called and
given an ovation, as was but just, but it was
cruel to the poet.

   " Withdraw the play at once," said Salemberry to Jacques Alençon.

   " Thank you, my dear sir, but you know——
When you bring me another tragedy, I shall
call in the police."

   Robert accompanied the ladies to the handsome house in the Rue de Bac, where Madame
de Fleurigny and her daughter were Madame
de Rillé's guests.

   As he took leave of them Gilberte held out
her hand to him, saying :

"You are depressed, are you not, M. de Salemberry?"

"No, Mlle. de Fleurigny, I am almost happy. Stephen is revenged."

Robert was not so happy as he said he was. The next morning's papers were more cruel than the public. "The Cid's Error" expiated the success of "The Poisonous Fang." Most of the critics decided that the chivalrous and historical drama had received its death-blow this time. Two or three of the more considerate judges protested against the public verdict; a week afterward it was no longer thought of.

The day after the disaster, Robert de Salemberry met one of his friends on the Boulevard.

"My dear fellow," said his friend, "the public was wrong—there are admirable things in that piece; if you will allow me, in ten years I shall rearrange the play and it will have an immense success."

"How, I pray you?"

Robert soon after this secured a delightful revenge. He published the second part of his grand poem, and the manner of its reception ought to have consoled the poet; but there is

no consolation for an unsuccessful play.   Such
varied experiences of humiliating disappointment and gratified pride must tell upon the
finest mind and the strongest constitution.
Robert fell ill, and the physicians ordered the
rest and quiet of home life.   He returned to
his aunt at Rillé, where he again met Madame
de Fleurigny and Gilberte.

CHAPTER X.

THE LETTER "G" AND "THE LAKE."

THE last months of winter were very dreary to our wounded hero, who, though triumphant, still felt the moral wound he had received. These favorites of fortune can ill endure the sudden rigors of fate. Robert was seized with a sort of feverish dejection and profound melancholy, accompanied by mental and physical prostration. Disgust and weariness of life were slowly consuming his strong nature. The failure of his play, in wounding his self-love, touched the most secret and noblest depths of his heart; before this catastrophe he cherished the hope of presenting his work as a retraction of his offence against Stephen; he would have liked to have dedicated to him his successful drama, but there is no homage in the dedication of an unsuccessful play. His hopes in this respect were sadly frustrated.

Besides, he believed it had lessened him in Gilberte's estimation; he compared himself to a blind lion he once saw in an Algerian village, serving as a plaything for the Arab children.

In addition to all this, the painful experience at the theatre had a terrible effect upon the poet physically. At decisive moments, in the instant when the battle may be lost or won, the pulsation of the heart is momentarily suspended, and thus it contracts the germs of future hypertrophy.

This hypertrophy of the heart was what Robert was threatened with. The illness was long and painful, and absolute rest was advised. But the imagination cannot rest like the body, and the unhappy poet had constantly in his mind the remembrance of those last few months, especially that fatal representation, and the dull eyes of that large, cold audience were always before him.

As may be imagined, every care was lavished upon him. His aunt, as well as Madame de Fleurigny and Gilberte, surrounded him with the most tactful and most ingenious attentions. Gilberte was celebrated in the country for her skill as a nurse, and this was not an occasion to refuse to exercise it. Nature aiding, the physical malady was soon conquered, but the moral ailment was more obstinate. With restored health Robert experienced only the painful weariness and anguish of bitter memories. His heart was healed, but empty.

One day while alone in the drawing-room. lying on a couch, he vainly sought to banish these gloomy ideas by watching the bright March sun pouring in through the wide-open door.

"What beautiful weather," he said to himself, "but what is it to me? Valentine de Milan was right: '*Rien ne m'est plus, plus ne m'est rien.*'" *

Suddenly Gilberte appeared in the warm, brilliant sunbeams that streamed through the door. She had just returned from the park, animated by her brisk walk, and on entering the room went directly toward Robert with head erect, smiling, and radiant as the aureole of sunbeams that surrounded her.

* "I am of interest to no one, and nothing is of interest to me."

Robert, rising, eagerly started forward to meet her, but staggered and was obliged to lean his trembling hands against the wall for support.

" What is the matter? " she asked.

" Oh, nothing, nothing."

" How pale you are.   Do you still suffer? "

" No, no.   I am quite well, quite."

And he closed his eyes to retain the thought of this heavenly vision.

It was almost heaven to him, for he was in love.

" I am looking for your aunt and my mother. Where are they? "

" Down there, on the bank of the pond. "

" I am going to join them, and shall bring them back to you."

" May I not accompany you, Mlle. Gilberte? "

" No; the March sun is still dangerous for you.   Sit there a little in the shade, like a prudent invalid, and wait for us."

Robert watched her as she went away, and his whole soul accompanied her.

" Yes, I love her, it is true.   I love her.   O my God, how good thou art!   How long I have loved her, I know not; whether it is within the last instant or for years. What matters it? I love her, I shall tell her mother and my aunt, and I shall declare my love to her, and we shall be married. But first I must write to Stephen."

Suddenly the young man's brow became clouded.

"Write to Stephen, her brother, whom I so basely outraged, and ask for the hand of his sister! Is it what he or she would be likely to wish? I remember the dreadful things she said to me that day, and even then, yes, on that very day I began to love her. How beautiful she was, as the lightning-flashes of her eyes lit up her brow. But I cannot hope to marry her; I was the cause of Stephen's losing the one he loved, and shall I say to him now: 'Give me your sister'? Impossible!

"Yes, it is impossible for the present; but later things will arrange themselves. Time is the accomplice of those who really love. I will work, now my heart is all aflame; I will work to become illustrious among the illustrious; I will heap poems upon dramas, Pelion upon

Ossa, and scale the heights of genius! And then I shall say to her: 'It is for you that I have done all this; I have made the world resound with my name, that I might offer it to you!' And I am sure that then—grant it, O my God—I am sure on that day she will not reject me."

Robert, with his poetic imagination, set to work to form his plan of conduct.

"Of course, I shall say nothing of this to her, or to any one. I shall talk to her as to all other women, simply and naturally, that she may suspect nothing. I shall envelop her in imperceptible tenderness. I shall give her name to a star and contemplate it in mute adoration, and the star will know nought of it."

Robert kept his word, and devised for himself the choicest pleasures. This highly wrought temperament loved like a child, found the most exquisite happiness in the veriest trifles; with a childishness of heart he found mysterious pleasure in artless, timorous attentions; little triumphs of concealed love in sublime efforts to pick up, unobserved, a glove that had fallen.

Our poet obtained two of these triumphs that made him forget the success of his finest works:

One day when Robert was sitting beside Gilberte on a bench in the park, not far from the porch where her mother and his aunt sat chatting, an irresistible desire came to his mind to make the young girl write her Christian name, Gilberte, in the sand, with the end of her parasol.

This is the first idea of lovers. Madame Swetchine says: "To write in pencil is to speak in a low voice." To write one's name in the sand is equal to speaking in a low voice or to signing a note of exchange on the future without knowing the nature of the note. This is why Robert longed to see Gilberte's name written by herself in the golden sands.

But how accomplish this thing, so easy or so difficult according as occasion offers? There are many ways, but Robert knew of only one: he must appeal solely to her imagination.

This is what this great poet, this composer of dramas, this inventor of grandiose scenes, considered the best way to effect the object of his desires.

After a long, silent meditation, he suddenly said to Gilberte:

"Mlle. de Fleurigny, I should not like to be called Gontran!"

"Why not?" asked the young girl, much astonished.

"Because the name Gontran begins with a *G.*"

"Well, what misfortune is there in that?"

"The misfortune is that the letter *G* is very difficult to write."

"Why the letter *G* more than all the others?"

"Because it is very complicated, and has rather an odd appearance. In fact, I have never been able to write it correctly, so as to look well."

"That astonishes me, M. de Salemberry, for there is nothing simpler."

"I should like to see a proof of it."

"You shall see."

And with the end of her white parasol Gilberte wrote the letter *G* in the fine sand.

"See!"

"You are right, Mlle. de Fleurigny, you are right. But there is another letter in the name

Gontran which I have still greater difficulty in writing; that is the letter *o;* my *o* looks like *a.* It is not as easy to write as the letter *i*, for example."

" You are mistaken again, M. de Salemberry; the letter *i* is very difficult."

" I should not have thought so."

"Certainly. The letter *i* has a straight stroke which requires the most careful attention, and it is quite an art to place the dot at the exact required distance. Look."

The young girl again wrote, with the end of her parasol tracing the letter *i* in the sand.

" You certainly have done it most perfectly."

She smiled, and, without further remark, finished writing her name, " Gilberte." Then she reassumed that profound, impenetrable expression that Robert knew so well, but which she had abandoned of late.

" Now, M. de Salemberry, could you tell me why you were so bent upon making me write my name here in the sand? "

" I, Mlle. de Fleurigny," answered Robert, blushing like a schoolboy. " Do you think I was bent upon it? Not at all, not at all; it was chance."

"The explanation is very clear, sir."

Another of Robert's fancies was to make Gilberte sing "The Lake," by Lamartine.

Poets, as a rule, are not particularly fond of music, unless they happen to be in love with the musician.

Women made a poor exchange in giving up the lute, the guitar, and, above all, the harp, for the piano. We should not like to make enemies among the fair sex, but we humbly confess that the prettiest woman in the world when playing the piano resembles a type-setter picking out the letters from the different compartments of his case. But to a heart deeply enamoured the woman loved is always beautiful, even when playing the piano; which does not prevent our regretting the time when the blond or brunette musician, standing beside a grand harp with golden strings, resembled one of Ossian's heroines.

One evening while Madame de Fleurigny and Madame de Rillé were receiving a visit from a rich farmer in the little reception-room, Gil-

berte remained alone with Robert in the drawing-room, and seated herself at the piano to
entertain him. She played moderately well, be
it said to her credit, but she had an admirable
voice, one of those mellow voices which seem
as though bathed in heavenly dew in passing
through the soul.

She had just sung "The Valley," by Lamartine, which in Gounod's exquisite music glides
like a gentle river flowing through the cool,
shady meadows. To hear "The Valley" sung
by one we love is very pleasant, but there is
something better; that is "The Lake."

Every verse of "The Lake" has made hun-
dreds of marriages; a number of them ought to
make millions.

> "Regarde : je vien seul m'asseoir sur cette pierre
> Où tu la vis s'asseoir."

"*Où tu la vis s'asseoir*" has married at least
two thousand English maidens.

> "Ainsi le vent jetait l'ecume de tes ondes
> Sur ses pieds adorés."

These two lines have made still greater legitimate havoc.

12

As to the concluding strophe of the last verse—

" Tout dise : Ils ont aimé,"

no further comment is necessary.

Robert said to himself : " 'The Valley' will certainly suggest to her the idea of 'The Lake' " ; but not at all.   Gilberte went with a bound to " Gastibelza," music by Monpou.   Robert held a grudge against Victor Hugo for this.

" I must have 'The Lake,' " he thought.

But after " Gastibelza " Gilberte tried a romance by Massenet.

" I must have 'The Lake,' and I will."

And Robert employed this primitively diplomatic means :

" Mlle. de Fleurigny, have you read the commentaries written by Lamartine himself, on 'The Meditations ' ? "

" No, M. de Salemberry."

" Well, this is what Lamartine says *à propos* of 'The Lake' : 'Of the thousand attempts made to add the plaintive melody of music to the sighing of these strophes, one only has succeeded.   Niedermeyer has touchingly translated this ode into music, and I have seen

tears flow when this romance was sung; nevertheless, I have always thought that poetry and music, when combined, mar each
other.' That is rather disdainful; do you not
think so?"

"Somewhat, I think."

"Have you there this romance of Niedermeyer's?"

"Oh, yes."

But Gilberte began to sing an old romance
of Loïsa Puget's. There was no further question of "The Lake," and Robert was in despair.

The next day, at the same hour, in the same
room, the marquise said to Gilberte:

"My dear child, a little music for the poor
prisoner."

Gilberte went to the piano, and, looking
archly at Robert in a way not at all habitual to
her, she began in a most marvellously sweet
voice:

" Ainsi toujours poussés vers de nouveaux rivages."

It was "The Lake."

"She has studied it since yesterday; her

self-love prompted that," thought Robert, who believed that he understood young girls' hearts.

Robert lived for several months upon such childish pleasures. May God deign to grant similar happiness to the greatest men of this world, if they deserve it!

CHAPTER XI.

ROBERT had some unhappy hours also. He was called upon to fulfil a difficult diplomatic mission against which his heart rebelled. Gilberte had been invited to wedding-festivities at a neighboring castle. It was an occasion of the greatest importance, and her mother asked Madame de Rillé to come and preside at Gilberte's toilette.

Robert accompanied his aunt to the house, and, while the ladies were collaborating over this piece of worldly vanity, the young girl's toilette, he remained alone in the drawing-room. It was not unpleasant to him to see Gilberte going to a dinner in full ball-dress, but he did not like the idea of seeing her only for a moment, and then not again for the rest of the day and evening; he had just then a number of important things to say to her, and he had formed an ingenious plan to secure a repetition of "The Lake." And this festivity comes and upsets everything.

"I am wrong," thought Robert, "I am wrong; it is good for a young girl to have amusement occasionally; she leads the life of the cloister here. I must not be selfish and exacting; I am very glad she is going to have a little diversion—I am very glad."

Gilberte entered the room all in white, wearing a necklace of pearls, a white rose in her golden hair, carrying a white fan in her hand. Robert was dazzled, but at heart he was furious. He noticed that her dress, which was cut too low according to his opinion, exposed to view the rosy mother-of-pearl like beauty of her delicate shoulders, and a multitude of tragic ideas crossed his mind.

"The present fashions are silly and indecent. A young girl ought not to wear such a low-necked dress, and in the province, too. That is well enough in Paris, for Paris sets the fashion; very soon there will be no province. It is the fault of the newspapers, that are paid by the dressmakers and milliners. It is the fault of the Empire that puts these ideas of luxury into women's heads. Will nothing change them? Governments imitate one another; it is not worth while to have a Republic."

Notwithstanding these social and political reflections, Robert's countenance cleared a little when he saw Gilberte throw over her shoulders an opera-cloak which completely enveloped her; the swansdown border encircled the young girl's pensive face like a jewel-casket. The parting smile Gilberte bestowed upon Robert as she drove off with her mother in the carriage was jealously treasured by him, but did not prevent his asking his aunt, when he returned to the house, a number of singular questions, such as :

" Will there be any officers at this wedding-reception ? "

" Probably, my dear nephew. General d'Acérac, who commands the division at Tours, is invited with all his staff."

" Really, aunt, this is why military men do not learn their profession."

During the evening of this unlucky day Robert's thoughts became more and more melancholy. He ought not, however, be too

much blamed for this.   It is not particularly
pleasant to know that the young girl we love is
at a ball, to think of her enjoying a feast in
which we have no part, through all the phases
of which we follow her with anxious interest,
and with jealousy all the more poignant that
she knows nothing of it.

" During dinner all goes well; there is something unavoidably grave and solemn in a wedding-feast.   Conversation is left to the serious
members of the company, and generally glides
into politics.   But after dinner there is the
ball, with the quadrilles, the mazurka, the waltz,
and that infamous cotillon! Gilberte is sure
to be surrounded; she does not waltz; no, certainly not; but the quadrille is allowed.   I
should really like to know why the quadrille is
allowed?   As to the cotillon, that invention
of the evil one, it is the staff officer's triumph.
And the cotillon always begins very late, when
the night air is coolest and pours in through
the windows left open by imprudent people;
there is the real danger.   Gilberte may return
with pleurisy, and she will suffer cruelly and
perhaps may die of it."

These were some of the gloomy thoughts
that surged like waves through Robert's brain.
Madame de Rillé noticed his preoccupation, and
about nine o'clock in the evening said to him,
smiling:

"You are rather Ossianesque,* my dear
nephew; would you like to hear some music,
by way of diversion? Shall I sing 'The Lake'
for you?"

"'The Lake'! I shall be delighted, dear aunt."

Madame de Rillé's voice was still fresh, and
she sang with much taste and feeling. But
neither the words nor the music touched
Robert's heart. To him "The Lake" was Gilberte. He praised his aunt's singing, however,
and, earnestly thanking her, retired to his own
room.

The next morning, at a very early hour, he
went to inquire for Madame de Fleurigny and
her daughter.

Gilberte was already in the garden, her countenance showing no signs of fatigue, her eyes

---

* Ossian is a legendary hero, chiefly known from Mac-
pherson's "Poems of Ossian." These poems are rather of a
gloomy character; hence the word "Ossianesque."

bright and smiling, and her voice full and musical as ever; there was no fear of pleurisy.

"You come to inquire for my mother, M. de Salemberry? Thank you; she is sleeping like one of the blessed."

"And you, Mlle. de Fleurigny?"

"Oh, I am, as you see, much less fatigued than I thought I should be."

"And what of the ball, this famous ball?"

"Well, I enjoyed myself."

"Indeed," said Robert, with a very dissatisfied air.

"Yes, and then I was dreadfully bored."

"Dreadfully? really, Mlle. de Fleurigny?"

"Yes, the cotillon was interminable."

"You had to leave before the end?"

"I wanted to very much, but it was impossible; I'll not be inveigled into it again."

"I am distressed to hear that you were so bored, Mlle. Gilberte."

He was radiant.

This was a red-letter day for our hero. She was bored at a ball! He hurried home to tell this piece of news to Madame de Rillé, who asked him coldly:

"Do you believe that, my dear nephew?"

"Certainly, aunt."

"Then youth has changed very much. In my time we were never bored at a ball."

"Possibly, but Gilberte is a person——"

"Superior, no doubt; thank you for the compliment you pay me."

"I only meant to say that worldly pleasures have no attraction for her—nothing more."

"If that is the case, I am almost sorry. Love of pleasure should be natural at her age. If a young girl is too serious she is apt, sooner or later, to take things very tragically."

"What a paradox, aunt."

"Reflect upon it, my dear nephew, and you will see that it is founded on truth."

"I shall, my dear aunt."

He did not reflect upon it at all, contenting himself with the thought of Gilberte's being bored at a ball when he was not present. This conviction sufficed his happiness for several days. Gilberte seemed drawn nearer to him by thus withdrawing herself from worldly pleasures, and he, forgetting the realities of life, slept in this sweet dream as the eagles are said to sleep hovering in the sun's rays in mid-air.

The awakening from such dreams is sometimes terrible.

One day Robert received a most unexpected visit from General d'Acérac. The general charged upon the young poet as he formerly attacked and carried by storm the Malakoff Tower.

" M. de Salemberry, you were the cause of my daughter Isabelle's not marrying Stephen de Fleurigny."

" General, you recall a memory very painful to me."

" I admire you. But as for him, I confess, between ourselves, that in Stephen's place I should have run you through the body as I would a rabbit; but he is a philosopher. Let that pass. I have a son as well as a daughter. Alexander saw Mlle. de Fleurigny at a ball last week, and he insists upon my asking her in marriage for him."

" Mlle. Gilberte!" exclaimed Robert.

" Exactly. Let us proceed to facts. These are my son's circumstances: a captain of cuirassiers, twenty-nine years of age, black hair, smooth face, delicate, firm hands, five feet eight (old measure), a slight scar on the left cheek, and a kind heart. You will want to know, of course, what fortune he has?"

"No, general, I do not care to know that."

"I shall tell you, all the same. At my death Alexander will have in my right the sword that I broke in the body of a Prussian officer at Borny. That is something. Besides, he has now already in right of his poor mother an income of 100,000 francs. As Mlle. de Fleurigny has only a small fortune, this will suit very well."

"But, general," stammered Robert, "I do not see how I can serve you in this affair."

"You can serve me by making my request known to Madame de Fleurigny and her daughter."

"I, general!"

"Exactly. Your aunt, Madame de Rillé, I am told, is an intimate friend of Madame de Fleurigny's; and it is said that you, sir, have a great influence over Mlle. Gilberte's mind since the appearance of that last drama of yours, 'The

Cid's Error,' which, in spite of public opinion, is a fine play, but understood only by military men like myself."

"That is sufficient honor for me, general."

"In short, and seriously, M. de Salemberry, you and I owe some reparation to the de Fleurigny family. Through your fault I refused to give my daughter to that good Stephen; I shall not refuse to give my son to the daughter, if she will.have him. It is my duty, and it is yours to aid me in accomplishing it."

"Very well, general," replied Robert in a quavering voice, "I shall execute the commission with which you charge me."

"Exactly. I shall expect your answer to-morrow."

"You shall have it, general."

"You understand it all, do you not? The sword in the Prussian's body, 100,000 francs income, five feet eight, and a kind heart. Do not forget his name—Alexander."

"I shall forget nothing, general."

"Exactly."

And with this, his habitual rejoinder, the general left Robert to his sad reflections, which

almost overwhelmed him. The blood surged
so violently through his heart he really feared
he would die. A thunderbolt had shattered
his dream, but the dreamer did not die of the
shock.

"That will be later," he said to himself;
"now I have but one thing to do, obey the
general's orders. He is right, it is my duty.
Moreover, if I do not do it the general will seek
some other intermediary—that is all. And
what would be thought of my refusal? What
right have I to refuse? It is quite enough to
have wrecked the brother's happiness without
now interfering with the sister's. After all,
this marriage will, no doubt, bring her happiness and good fortune. Yes, happiness with
another. If I wished, however, I could prevent her accepting this offer. I could explain
to her that she could not, ought not, to enter
a family from which her brother was almost
driven. This is a reason against, as well as
for, the marriage; it is, in one sense, a reparation, as the general says, but, on the other hand,
it is a new affront to Stephen. They are very
willing to have his sister, but they would not

have him. I could tell her this and a hundred
other things. Marrying an army officer is
really very hazardous, and prudent mothers
would much rather keep their daughters than
expose them to such an uncertain future.
What would become of Madame de Fleurigny
deprived of her daughter? She would have
been a mother to me. But the real reason is
that I love Gilberte, and I do not wish her to
marry another. I think only of myself, and
that makes love cowardly; but what of her happiness? She, perhaps, will love this brave,
handsome young man, who is also rich and
noble, and could not see her without loving her.
Suppose she should marry some one else, who
would prove unworthy of her and make her
unhappy—one never knows what may happen.
Then this would be my own fault. Shall I be
the sister's executioner as well as the brother's?
That must not be! I will do my duty; I will
go and tell her all, and say, such is the man
who offers himself to you. She will accept
him, of course, and I shall advise her to do so,
if necessary. I sought to repair the injury I inflicted and I did not succeed, but God now sends

me this means of reparation. It will be happiness for her, but death to me. Oh, yes! and I hope and feel assured that death will not long be delayed."

A quarter of an hour later Robert was with Gilberte. In a calm voice, but with a pale countenance, he repeated all that the general had just said to him. Gilberte listened in silence, fastening upon him that vague, fixed look of which we have so often spoken; then, leading him up to Stephen's portrait, she said slowly:

"In the name of your friend Stephen, M. de Salemberry, what do you advise me?"

"In Stephen's name, Mlle. de Fleurigny, I advise you to marry M. d'Acérac."

And Robert's face became livid.

"I will not marry M. d'Acérac nor any one else."

"Why, Mlle. Gilberte?"

"Because you love me, Robert, and because I love you."

"O Gilberte, I shall die of joy!"

"Stay, Robert. I love you, but I will never marry you. Listen to me, and you will then

13

see that I am right.   I have always loved you.
I cannot remember the time when I did not
love you.   I know not why I love you, and I
have never sought to discover.   I only know
that when you were here I was happy; when
you spoke to us of poetry and art I watched
you, listened to you, and my soul revelled as in
a feast.   Once only I was alarmed about you.
You had climbed to the top of that old stone
gate of which our village is so proud, you know;
it can be seen from here.   Suddenly you became dizzy.   'He is going to fall,' cried
Stephen, running to your assistance.   And I
thought I should have died.   I discovered on
that day that I loved you.   Do you doubt it,
Robert?"

"No, Gilberte; unfortunately, no."

"It is true; if you had known how I loved
you, you would not have done what you did to
Stephen.   When I heard it, when my mother,
weeping bitterly, told me that dreadful thing,
when Stephen, pale as you are this moment,
told me of his life's happiness wrecked forever,
of his love disdained on account of your wicked
deed, it seemed as though the earth opened

under my feet, and that I was about to be swallowed up in an abyss. How bitterly I execrated you that day! On my knees, with tears of rage, I begged God to avenge my brother, and to punish you; and I loved you through it all. But I was ashamed of it, and I felt, with horrible despair, that what I resented most in your wicked act was the suffering it caused me. Must I confess it? I almost blamed Stephen to justify you. I said to myself, 'He ought not to have been too proud to give you proof of his innocence; he should have foreseen and prevented all this.' Yes, I censured that gentle martyr, my brother. This is to me, Robert, the most grievous part of your unworthy deed. You have made my soul blush, but I am also to blame, and I must make expiation."

" You, Gilberte ! "

" Yes, Robert, both of us—I, as well as you; we were both to blame. Let us unite in expiating our fault. Stephen wept over his shattered love; we will weep over the ruin of ours."

" I bow submissively to the justice of my richly deserved misery. But you, Gilberte ? "

"Do not seek to dissuade me, Robert; you will not succeed; my resolution is taken."

"Will nothing move you, Gilberte? If you really loved me——"

"It is because I love you that I am going away."

"Going away!"

"Yes, I start to-morrow for Rome with my mother, where we shall join Stephen, whose prolonged absence astonishes us and makes us anxious."

"And when will you return, Gilberte?"

"I do not know."

"When you have conquered your love for me?"

"Never, then!"

"Never!"

"Yes, Robert, never! You see how necessary it is that I should go. *Adieu,*" she added, holding out to him a cold, trembling hand.

That same evening General d'Acérac received the answer he was awaiting:

"My dear General:

"I have not succeeded in the mission you did

me the honor to confide to me. Mlle. de Fleurigny does not wish to leave her mother.

"Accept, my dear general, etc.,

"Marquis Robert de Salemberry."

The general answered immediately:

"Sir:

"I thank you for having fulfilled the mission
I asked you to accept. I hold you in no way
responsible for its failure. Nevertheless, it
seems to me that a dramatic author ought to
succeed better in questions of marriage. Alexander is in despair, but he is a man and will
soon console himself; exactly.

"Receive, sir, etc.,

"General Count d'Acerac."

Gilberte and her mother left Rillé the next
morning.

CHAPTER XII.

THE most terrible trials are not those crushing sorrows that overwhelm and kill at a single blow; they are those the bitterness of which is not felt at first, but are borne in upon us gradually, and dishearten and unman us.

Robert did not, at first, fully realize the extent of his misfortune. These were the thoughts that predominated the agitation of his heart and soul: "She divined that I loved her, and she loves me; she knows that we love each other, the rest will adjust itself. Gilberte's exaltation, doubtless, will not last. Now she can take only one view of things; later, soon, she will see the other side. Hers is a deeply poetic soul, rather tragically poetic. She is too fond of Corneille, and has read 'The Cid' too much. She, like Chimène, coquettes with love and duty, and throws herself heroically

198

into the rôle of sacrifice; but, like Chimène, she requires but one word from the king who orders her to forgive Rodrigues."

Robert forgot that we are living in a republic.

The next day he strolled to the village, and went to Gilberte's house, the door of which the gardener opened for him.

"Well, Father Fulcran, the ladies went off yesterday?"

"Yes, sir."

"How did Madame de Fleurigny seem?"

"She seemed happy and very much pleased, sir. As she entered the carriage she said to Mlle. Gilberte, 'We shall soon see Stephen again, my darling.'"

"And what did Mlle. Gilberte say?"

"Nothing, sir. I am mistaken—she talked a little apart with Catalina, the wife of that gypsy, you know, a race of savages, and I caught, in passing, a few words of what she was saying to her: 'Above all, if M. Robert comes to hunt in the Lande.' I did not hear the rest, but I saw that Mlle. Gilberte slipped several gold pieces into Catalina's hand, which was money badly placed, with all respect to you, sir. Finally, just as they were leaving, I took the liberty of saying to the young lady, 'I hope you return soon, Mlle. Gilberte?' 'Soon! no, oh, no!' she replied, and a tear rolled down her cheek, and I thought, there is a brave girl who loves her country well."

"Thank you, Fulcran, thank you."

Robert remained alone in the deserted house. Who has not experienced the sadness that pervades the empty house that yesterday was filled with the voices, footsteps, friendly glances, and sweet presence of those who are gone?

As she sat there near the window, in the large tapestry-covered arm-chair, her dress falling in graceful folds over the old oaken footstool, she might have been taken for one of the chatelaines in Geste's ballads. She was embroidering a piece of fancywork, her figure erect, her head bent slightly forward, stopping occasionally to listen as the old clock in the neighboring church-tower struck the hour; she had a way of listening to the striking of the clock unlike other women. When she rose, the sound of her footsteps as she glided over the inlaid floor, and the rustle of her gown, as with a quick, almost impatient movement she closed or opened the window-curtains, were like sweet music. These are the things that cling to the memory. The little drawing-room seems like a great desert when she is no longer there; how cold and bare the house is without her; it may be better in the garden, but there it is still more lonely. The rustic grotto, where she loved to read, looks reproachfully at the intruder who dares to come without her. The little rivulet weeps for her, the turtle-doves do not recognize her former companion, and fly away as she has fled.

"I am to blame for all that has happened," thought Robert. "It was I who drove her from her home; she preferred exile to my presence, and there she is now exposed to all the dangers of a journey—fatigue, illness, fever, perhaps death!"

Robert buried his face in his hands, and shuddered at this idea. Leaving the garden he passed through the house, his heart full of forebodings.

This poignant anxiety lasted several days,

but it was, fortunately, relieved by Gilberte's letter to Madame de Rillé:

"ROME, November 17th.

"MADAME LA MARQUISE:

"I shall write you only a very short letter to-day.   We have scarcely been an hour in Rome, and we have just seen our dear Stephen. Mother and I enjoyed the journey very much; we were not in the least fatigued.   The rail-roads are too much maligned.   Stephen received us with his usual tenderness, which you so well know.   There is an indescribable something about him, a particularly happy air, which must come from something more than the pleasure of seeing us.   I scent a mystery; we shall see. Begging you to give our kind regards to M. Robert, I am, with love and respect, dear madame la marquise,

"GILBERTE DE FLEURIGNY.

"P. S.   Caution M. Robert to be very careful if he goes hunting in the neighborhood of the gypsies."

Gilberte's letter, showing that she was perfectly well, dispelled all Robert's fears. It contained, moreover, a sentence upon which our poet constructed a romance. What could be this mystery about Stephen, of which Gilberte speaks?

" If it were a marriage, if Stephen had finally found a beautiful Roman to console him! Yes, that is it, it must be that! Then there is hope for me; if Stephen is happy, Gilberte will no longer have any reason for persisting in her refusal, in her terrible resolution. Certainly, that is it."

With these thoughts Robert's imagination bounded to the most radiant horizon. But, unfortunately, the following extract from Gilberte's second letter diminished his enthusiastic hopes:

" Yes, madame la marquise, we have discovered Stephen's secret. There is nothing sentimental about the mystery. Every day Cardinal Beppo comes for Stephen and takes him to the Vatican, where His Holiness receives him in private audience. I asked my brother to what he owed such rare honor, and this is what he told me:

" Stephen has undertaken to write a history

of the first centuries of the Church. The Pope is deeply interested in this great work, and Stephen goes every day to the Vatican to confer with him on the subject. I confess that I imagined, not something better, but something quite different. The fact is, Stephen will never forget what you know as well as we. He will never marry, *any more than his sister.*"

Gilberte had underlined these last words.

"It evidently was for me," thought Robert, "and not for my aunt, that she underlined that last phrase; she wished to remind me of her unalterable resolution. This dispels my dream of happiness. *'Any more than his sister!'*"

And yet Robert continued to hope; it seemed to him impossible that Stephen's good advice, for he now knew how generous he was, could fail, with absence and separation, to have a better influence on the young girl's mind. Hope in the heart of a lover is like the roots of the oak, the depth of which exceeds the height of its branches. Robert always repeated to himself after his reveries: "Nothing is lost, life is long."

One morning Robert while walking in the park met the postman, who gave him the marquise's mail. On one of the letters, bearing the Naples stamp, he recognized Madame de Fleurigny's handwriting. Lovers have intuitions.

"Gilberte is ill!" exclaimed Robert to himself, as he ran breathlessly to the castle.

"Read this quickly, aunt. Gilberte is ill." He was not mistaken. This was the letter:

"NAPLES, November 28th.

"DEAR, KIND FRIEND:

"I am very anxious about Gilberte. She caught the marsh-fever at Rome, and we brought her away without a moment's delay. The physicians here have as yet given no opinion. Pray for my poor child.

"Your desperate friend,

"VICTORINE DE FLEURIGNY."

"She will die! Gilberte is dying, is perhaps dead already! Oh! aunt, you do not know that I love her, and that she loves me. If she dies I will kill myself."

"If I had only known! Come, my child, let us have recourse to God," said the marquise, and she went with her nephew to the little church at Rillé.

Robert was religious in mind and heart, but literary life, especially his theatrical works, had made him an indifferent Christian. When in the country he went to Mass for the sake of good example and to please his aunt. In Paris he went only to nuptial and requiem Masses. "That is always so much loss to the devil," he would say laughingly to his friends.

He did not laugh now. He went directly to the Blessed Virgin's altar, and, joining his hands, fell upon his knees, and poured forth a cry of lover and poet, in which the prayers of his childhood, recalled in fragments, were mingled with formulas and phrases of theatrical literature; but it was all spontaneous, simple, and sincere.

"Obtain, good Mother of Sorrows, that Gilberte may not die. Queen of Angels, obtain for me the life of this good angel. Consoler of the Afflicted, remember the night of Golgotha, and the arms of that tree dyed in the blood of thy Son. I love Gilberte and she loves me; let her not be taken from me, or take me with her. I have been proud and wicked; I will be good and humble now, and do all the good I can in the world; I take thy white veil, thy holy aureole, and the smile of the infant God whom thy hands hold out to those who weep, as silent witnesses of my vow.   Restore Gilberte to me, O my Mother!"

Robert rose from his prayer more calm, and returned with his aunt to the castle.   In the evening all his anguish revived, poetic memories mingled with his personal sorrow; Gilberte dying in *Graziella's* country recalled to his mind "The Coral Fisher," Lamartine's beautifully pathetic poem on "La Fille d'Ischia":

"In her first tear she drowned her heart!"

Gilberte also had drowned her heart in her first tear, and, since it was he who had caused that tear to flow, God should punish him, not Gilberte.

No sleep came to Robert's relief that night. Such sleepless nights fully expiate evil deeds. At early dawn he hurried to the post-office for the mail.   There were no letters, only a telegram:

"Gilberte is saved; there is no danger now.

"Ischia, December 1st.   Stephen."

Robert wept like a child, and returned, almost crazed with joy, to bring the good news to his aunt.

These illusive hopes, deceptive fears, bitter memories, and dreams of happiness, alternated repeatedly in Robert's heart since Gilberte's departure and illness, as if an invisible hand had doled out to him equal measures of hope and fear.

.   .   .   .   .   .

Early in March a son and heir was born to M. and Mme. de Nolongue, and Robert was godfather to this pink and white prodigy.

The intelligence shown by this new citizen, when only a week old, was doubtless due to heredity; a deputy's son ought to prove his patriotism by manifesting his intelligence at an early age. The first and strongest mark of intelligence he gave was his authoritative manner of asking for a drink, nor was he satisfied with the sugared water with which the frequenters of the Palais-Bourbon quench their thirst. A gesture sufficed, but it was so imperative that his mother never could resist the eloquent appeals, which were as much admired by the godfather as by the parents.

But history must not be falsified; the deputy's son acquired faults as he grew, and became gradually less angelic. For example, when he had completely gorged himself in satisfying his appetite, his gray eyes sparkling and his small face crimson with satisfaction, he showed his fist, revealing the future orator; he was already a good interrupter, for when his parents and godfather were chatting quietly together, while watching him smiling in his nurse's arms, he would suddenly interrupt these long conversations, of which he understood nothing, by bawling like one possessed.

This was intolerable. A call to order did not suffice, even censure was of no avail; then Louis de Nolongue, recalling the strict rules of the Chamber of Deputies, would cry out:

"*Au petit local, au petit local!*" *

The *petit local* was the silk and lace-trimmed

---

* A room near the senate-chamber to which, formerly, unruly members were banished when they interrupted the proceedings. The room still exists, though the custom has passed into disuse.—[TRANSLATOR.

cradle, a dainty nest that had been prepared for the arrival of the little bird, to which the mother carried the noisy interrupter. Under its influence the cries ceased as if by magic, and the offender immediately fell asleep. Here it was that he showed to best advantage; the fond parents and the godfather gazed upon him with admiration and delight, and it would be difficult to say which admired the most. The father's pride was a pleasure to behold, and, although Robert shared his cousin's happiness, yet he could not help envying it a little.

Poets are very fond of children. Great poets are made for the double paternity of men and thoughts; they have a peculiar ambition, a secret pride in transmitting their genius to posterity.

Robert had long cherished this proud ambition, and the sweet dream of seeing it realized; but he now felt convinced that his fond dream had forever vanished, and each day added to the bitterness of his regret. In spite of the envy aroused by his visits, he went regularly to watch his godson sleeping in his pretty cradle, *the petit local*, and chose the time when he could be alone with the prisoner.

That charming domestic picture, a sleeping child, is generally very soothing to a man. It was not so with Robert; the sight of this little rosy angel increased his envy, and he felt himself becoming more and more sad and desolate. Then he thought of Gilberte, who like him adored children, loved to fondle and caress them, and knew so well how to care for them, but who was never to know the august joy of motherhood, for, on account of his revengeful pride, she had condemned herself to forego this happiness.

This idea pursued Robert remorsefully; he tried in vain to escape it; the implacable goad was in the flesh, and he himself turned the iron in the wound with a sort of savage delight.

"I am destined to martyrize all who love me, the sister even more than the brother. There is a fatality about me that makes everything I touch crumble. My own life has been a failure, and I have wrecked the lives of others. Were I to go away, to disappear, if the hand of death were mercifully laid upon me, it would only be removing an evil thing. Who knows what harm I may yet do? My hands are full

of tempests, and the dark forger of evil works
in my breast. I have made Gilberte suffer,
and I shall cause her still more suffering. If
a ball from a poacher's gun should pierce my
skull in a lonely path, the poacher would render
me a service as well as others."

This idea of death, this thirst for a bloody
expiation crept gradually into Robert's mind
and took complete possession of his imagination. Poets, dreamers, those whose minds are
ill at ease, have a feverish curiosity about the
unknown. They are homesick for that land to
which the soul must one day go; and when at
night they eagerly contemplate the starry fir-
mament, each star is a magnet attracting them
thither. Robert had too noble, too religious a
soul to think of suicide. Moreover, it would
be a cause of reproach to him, as he would consider it an additional crime to leave Gilberte
such a horrible memory. No, he dreamed of a
noble, glorious death, in some great battle in defence of the country, on the bridge of a man-of-
war, shattered by bombs, or some battlefield in
Alsace or Lorraine, riddled with bullets. But
the sombre Angel of War has long since taken

flight, doubtless for too long a time. Those who wish to die must await God's good time.

Robert was anxious to die; he did not wish to kill himself, but he might expose himself to death, did timely occasion offer. A despatch from Langeais brought frightful news to the inhabitants of Rillé. The Loire had overflowed its banks, the dikes were broken above Langeais, and all the country was under water. Robert only took time to saddle his horse and rode off at a gallop.

At Langeais the scene was terrifying. The raging flood swept far out of sight, bearing on its seething waves the wreck of ruined towns and villages. Below Langeais a little hamlet was almost submerged beneath the foaming waters, and from the high ground and the castle towers, the inhabitants, who had taken refuge on the roofs of the houses, could be seen waving their arms in despair.

To attempt to save them seemed useless and foolhardy, even to the most venturous sailor and the most fearless life saver; but Robert sprang into a boat, unfastened the moorings, and launched out into the torrent.

"He is lost!" cried the crowd; but with great skill, strength, and extraordinary coolness he guided the boat towards the village, which he soon reached, borne on by the current. Dexterously catching the rope thrown to him from a window, he collected the frightened people in his small craft, and launched out again into the stream. The current, fortunately, carried the boat towards the nearest shore, and drove it upon the bank so rapidly and with such force that it stuck fast in the sand. The violent shock threw a child from its mother's arms into the water, and it was carried off on a wave. Robert immediately plunged into the flood, crying out "For Gilberte!" and swam desperately towards the child, which was disappearing. After a frantic struggle he succeeded in reaching the shore with his burden, where he fell, completely exhausted, and lay with closed eyes, perfectly unconscious and apparently lifeless.

But death would not claim him. In a few minutes Robert was restored to consciousness, and in the evening he returned to Rillé castle.

This thrilling incident, notwithstanding the satisfaction derived from a well-accomplished

duty, only increased Robert's depression. When
he was so near death it had seemed so sweet
to him, that his regret at having missed it was
greater than his desire for it had been, and he
sank into the deepest melancholy, dwelling for
long hours on the vision that appeared to his
excited imagination, as with closed eyes he lay
awaiting death. He believed that he saw Gilberte lean over him and press her lips to his
brow.

This memory clung to him in his continually
feverish state, and he still longed for death,
that he might see Gilberte once more, and again
feel upon his brow the caressing touch of those
adored lips.

The mind cannot long resist the baneful
effect of dwelling on the same thoughts, feel-
ings, and desires. Robert's relatives and friends
became alarmed at the change in his habits, and
often thought that the mournful sadness of his
countenance and his fixed gaze showed vague
signs of insanity.

One day, alone in his study, he sat mechani-
cally holding a book open on his knee, staring
steadily at an angle of the wall, deeply buried

in thought, and so absorbed in his profound meditation that he did not hear the door open, and only turned his head when he felt a hand laid on his shoulder.

It was a young priest who had entered, and with outstretched arms said to him, smilingly:

"Well, Robert, welcome your future pastor!"

"Stephen!"

They folded each other in an affectionate embrace, and then Stephen continued, in a graver tone:

"Listen to me, Robert. I wrote you, if you remember, that perhaps I should owe my happiness to you, and I was not mistaken. My heart was broken at one time, and the fragments were of no use in the world, but God was willing to accept them. I was not made for the storms of human passions, and I took refuge in great peace of soul. Thanks to you, I am a priest. You alone could expiate the fault you committed, and which you have now sufficiently deplored; the victim only could repair it. For three years I studied to improve my mind, and consulted my heart to learn if I

should be worthy of this new mission. The
Sovereign Pontiff deigned to consider me worthy, and was good enough to shorten for me
the time of probation, which is rarely done.
What Gilberte confided to my mother and to
me finally decided me to take this step."

"Gilberte! Oh, Stephen, do you know
then——"

"All that you have suffered for each other.
I reproved her for her excessive severity, and I
strongly disapproved of her inflexible resolution.
I have not yet been able to overcome her scru-
ples sufficiently to make her promise to be your
wife, but if she has not said *yes*, she has not, at
least, said *no*. Take courage, then, and let time
do its work. You show the effect of the terrible blow you have experienced. I pity you
from the bottom of my heart, and I long to
assuage your present suffering. I bless you
for the anguish you caused me in days gone by,
since it has given me to God."

Then Stephen, affectionately embracing Robert, continued in a familiar tone, his noble face
beaming with the pleasant smile habitual to
him:

"My great, illustrious friend, I shall denounce you to Gilberte."

"Why, Stephen—why?"

"You have not even asked where she is."

"I had not the courage, dear Stephen, but where is she?"

"Have you had no suspicion, my poor fellow? She is here, downstairs in the drawing-room with my mother and your aunt."

"Let us go down at once. But I am afraid. You will defend me, will you not, Stephen?"

.   .   .   .   .   .

At sight of Gilberte Robert seemed to recover himself completely. He suddenly felt all his strength of mind restored, all his genius awaken with the love that shone in his eyes and throbbed in his heart. After an interchange of cordial greetings with the mother and daughter, Robert was suddenly seized with an irresistible desire to show them his godson.

"Mlle. Gilberte," said he, with a smile that had been rare of late, "will you do me a favor— will you come with me to Les Chartrettes to see the *petit local* of my godson, Prosper de No-longue?"

" What is the *petit local?* "

" You will see."

They all set out together for Les Chartrettes. On the way fresh anxiety took possession of Robert's mind as to how he should persuade her to say yes.

When they arrived they found that Master Prosper de Nolongue had just been indulging in the noisiest of interruptions, and had been put in the *petit local;* Gilberte was amused at Robert's explanation of the affair.

The baby was in a deep sleep; his little breast rose and fell under the folds of its dainty dress, his hands clutched an ivory rattle, the bells of which were as silent as he, the soft lashes cast a light shadow on the delicate pink cheeks, his parted lips showing his rose-lined mouth. They all gazed upon this masterpiece with that respect due to a work of art, no one venturing to speak for fear of disturbing his slumber; but all eyes said plainly, " How beautiful!"

Robert, observing the softening influence this lovely spectacle of a sleeping angel had on Gilberte, determined to avail himself of it, and, throwing his whole soul into his pleading eyes, he raised them in mute appeal to hers.   Gilberte returned his gaze, her heart responded to his yearning glances, and she softly murmured, " Yes."

CHAPTER XIII.

THE LAST SONNET.

THE marriage was celebrated in the little church at Rillé. Stephen claimed the right of giving Gilberte and Robert the nuptial blessing. Only the relatives and most intimate friends were invited; but they reckoned without the Paris papers. Pierre Robès, always fully informed of everything, gave the signal by an article in *The Viper*—a very respectful article, however, showing no little emotion. The other papers not wishing to be outdone, there appeared about sixty articles full of singular and contradictory details. The railroad organized a marriage-train, and Robert was surprised to find all the *élite* of Paris in the little church at Rillé. This did not, however, disturb him very much, for the bride was fair to see, and he did not object to her being seen.

Stephen, in the presence of this unexpected audience, escaped, by the simplicity of his bearing and manner, a situation which might have been embarrassing. He spoke to the young bride and groom as a priest very seriously, and as a brother with a tenderness and affection that brought tears to the eyes of even the reporters, who are not usually given to weeping.

The wedding-breakfast was given by the good Marquise de Rillé at the castle.

Since his return Stephen had felt that the best way of showing Robert that he had forgotten the past was by casually referring to it. With this intention he occasionally reminded Robert of what he called their " illustrious quarrel," and he finally succeeded in making Robert join with him in laughing at it, by quietly teasing him from time to time about that celebrated " Poisonous Fang,"—" the spirit of which amounts to no more than the title," he would pleasantly add; so that after a while Robert rather relished the kindly epigrams of his intended victim, and finally came to the conclusion that he himself was decidedly the victim now; in which opinion Gilberte to a certain extent agreed with him.

At the end of the repast Stephen rose, smiling, and made the following little speech:

"My dear brother-in-law Robert, you shall not escape even on this occasion. This is a sonnet; I have written many of them in my youthful days; history relates that they did not all meet with your approbation. This one will be my last:

> " 'Tis the last sonnet I shall ever write,
> And for my recompense my friend shall say
> What merit in my verse—for who, I pray,
> May better tell or with a clearer sight?
> As late I wandered in the crescent light
> And lessening shadows of the morning gray,
> And heard the wild bird's music by the way,
> No tear, I said, nor shadow from the night,
> Should cloud the splendor of a day so bright
> In promise and fulfilment. May the best
> Of all things wait thee. Journey forth, I pray,
> Genius and grace in happy union blest,
> To the far portals of the endless day,
> With fame and bliss unclouded, and have rest."

Stephen, seeing that the tears in Robert's eyes were about to overflow, said:

"Well, Robert, what do you think of my last sonnet? If you think it poor, do not, at least, say so in public."

"Stephen, you always were a tease," answered Robert, smiling.

About ten o'clock the Marquise de Rillé took Robert aside, and said in a mysterious manner:

"My dear nephew, I have a present to make you, to say nothing of my fortune."

"What present, my dear aunt?"

"I give you the 'Game of Virtues,' to which, you know, you, to a certain extent, owe your happiness."

"I accept, but I do not see it in the drawing-room as usual. Where is it, my dear aunt; where has it been put?"

The marquise, with that merry smile habitual to her on occasions of this kind, said:

"Where is 'The Game of Virtues'? Can you not guess where it has been put?"

"No, cruel aunt!"

"What sublime simplicity! In your room."

.   .   .   .   .   .

All the characters of this story are equally happy, although unequally deserving.

Louis de Nolongue, now the happy father of twins, continues to pity his predecessor, the late M. Morel, who had no children.

Pierre Robès, while continuing as journalist, still makes repeated theatrical ventures; one of his plays is hissed every three months, but this does not prevent the managers asking him for others. This is done as a medical precaution, so to speak. Robès' plays turn the bad humor of the public on him alone; they are played for the same reason that we have ourselves vaccinated and re-vaccinated—to carry off the bad humors.

The manager of *The Viper* is senator; he has changed the name of his paper, which is now called *The Antidote.* Unfortunately, *The Antidote* has a very small circulation.

Maria Orfano, the great, noble actress, has given up the stage. She left France to marry a Russian—Sebastopol's revenge.

Jacques Alençon is Minister of Fine Arts, which gives him an opportunity of adequately tormenting his former *confrères*, the theatrical managers.

15

Finally, the Marquise de Rillé is godmother to Gilberte's first-born, and she heroically declares that she will be godmother to all that may follow.

www.ingramcontent.com/pod-product-compliance
Lightning Source LLC
Chambersburg PA
CBHW030321270326
41926CB00010B/1457